THE CONVERT'S PASSION

Borgo Press Books by Brent D. Singleton

Yankee Muslim: The Asian Travels of Mohammed Alexander Russell Webb

THE CONVERT'S PASSION

An Anthology of Islamic Poetry from Late Victorian and Edwardian Britain

Edited by

Brent D. Singleton

THE BORGO PRESS

An Imprint of Wildside Press LLC

MMIX

Copyright © 2009 by Brent D. Singleton

All rights reserved.
No part of this book may be reproduced in any form
without the expressed written consent
of the author and publisher.
Printed in the United States of America

www.wildsidepress.com

FIRST EDITION

CONTENTS

INTRODUCTION AND ACKNOWLEDGEMENTS 11

AHMED C(URTIS) BRANN

There Is No God But Thee 17

W(ILLIAM) OBEID-ULLAH CUNLIFFE

Truth 19
The Orient Sun of Islam 19
Wad-El-Nejumi's Charge at Tosti 20
The Creed of Truth 21
Sow Islam's Seed! 22
The Moslimah's Jewels 23
The Hajee 24
Sands 25
The Dawn of Faith 26
A Moslem's Prayer 27
The Alms of Aziz 28
Ibrahim's Sin 29
The Enchanted Fallen 31
The Thief, Old Time 33
Life! 34

VALFRID "FRIIDI" HEDMAN

The Sisterhood of Languages 37

The Muslim's Heaven 43
To the Materialistic Christian 43
Stray Lines 43
The Rose of Sharon 44
The Nirvana 45

HENRI MUSTAPHA LÉON

Victoria 46
The Two Foes 47

AMEENAH (EMILY) LINCOLN

La Illa Ha, Illa Allah! 49
Hope Delusive! 50
Indian Trees 51
The Suleiman Stone (The Opal) 52
The Palm Tree on the Dublin Mountains at Newbrook,
  Rathfarnham 53
The Fort Agra! 54

YEHYA-EN-NASR (JOHN) PARKINSON

Zengi 57
The Spirit of God 62
Zola 63
The Dirge We Dirging Dree 64
The Song of the Despondent Lover 65
Ez Zegri 66
An Inspiration 68
With Apologies to Sheik Abdullah Quilliam Effendi,
  Sheikh-ul-Islam 69
A Ballad of Chivalry 70
On the Dee 71
Love-Dreams 72
Jemal-ud-deen Bokhari Jeffery 73
In the Gloom 74

Almansur (1) 75
Verses 76
The Poet's Dream 77
A Dream 78
Muslim Battle-Song 79
H.I.M. Abdul-Hamid Ghazi Khan, Sultan of Turkey, Emir-el-
   Mumooneen 80
Almansur (2) 83
To His Excellency W.H. Abdullah Quilliam Bey Effendi 85
The Last Great Moor 85
I Sat By the Wayside Alone 91
Abdallah Ez Zagal at Fez 93
The Clarion of Islam 96
To His Imperial Majesty Ghazi Abdul-Hamid Khan Sultan of
   Turkey, Emir-el-Mumooneen 97
[Untitled] (1909) 101

SAMUEL (SAMI) PIGEON

[Untitled] (1898) 102
A Laudatory Ode 103

SHEIKH W(ILLIAM) H(ENRY) ABDULLAH QUILLIAM

An Isha Prayer 105
Moslem Morning Hymn 105
In Memoriam (William Obeid-Ullah Cunliffe) 107
The Moslem's Refuge 108
Scale Force 109
The Triumph of Truth 110
The Lessons of Experience 111
Maxims for Muslims 112
Circumstances Alter Cases 113
Thoughts for Thinkers 115
To a Child Playing with Toy Bricks 116
Which of Them Was Neighbour Unto Her? 117
True Pleasures 118

Hope On! Hope Ever!!	119
A Gem from Saadi	120
A Muslim Prayer	121
Hymn for the Prophet's Birthday	121
Waiting	122
The Key to Happiness	124
The True Easter	125
A Janaaza Ode to the Muslim Warriors Who Fell in the Greco-Turkish War	127
The Muslim's Evening Prayer	128
"Oh Death! Where Is Thy Sting?"	129
The Angel Message	130
Ode to the Memory of General Ghazi Hafiz Pasha	131
A Vision of Paradise	132
Islamic Resignation (1)	134
To My Son, R. Ahmed Quilliam Bey, on the 19th Anniversary of His Birthday	135
The Death of Abdullahi	137
The Last Journey	138
Night Thoughts	139
Our Departed Friends	140
A Plea in Abatement	141
Ode to Scandal-Mongers	142
The Death of the Old Year	143
A Muslim Hymn	144
A Muslim Anthem	144
The Witnesses	145
The Gateway of the Grave	146
Some Good Advice to Single Men	147
In Memoriam (Bro. Jemal-ud-deen Bokhari Jeffery)	148
A B C (All Best Come)	149
The Riddle of Life	152
Nil Desperandum!	154
Islamic Resignation (2)	154
Ode to "The Autocrat of all the Russias"	155
Kindliness	156
The Onward Path	157

After Many Years 127
What Is Life? 158

S. AMINA RIDGWAY

Ismail 159

HENRY YUTE JONES TAYLOR (H.Y.J.T.)

To Abdul Hamid, Sultan of Turkey (1) 161
To Abdul Hamid, Sultan of Turkey (2) 161
Sonnet 162
Our Lady Chapel 163

AMHERST D(ANIEL) TYSSEN

The Caliph Ali's Hymn 165
Hymn on Mohammed in the Cave 166
Hymn on the Welcome to Medina 167
Hymn (The Signs of God) 168
Hymn on the Purpose of Creation 169
On Immortality 170
An Appeal to Christians 171
The Battle of Bedr 172
Hymn on the Faith of Abraham 173
Hymn—Who is the Pious Moslem? 174
Hymn on the Capture of Mecca 175
Evening Hymn 176
The Natural Rules of Duty 177
The Prophet's Resolution 179
Summer Holidays 180
Hymn on Almsgiving from the Koran 181

ANONYMOUS, INITIALS, UNKNOWN PSEUDONYMS

New Christian Anthem 182
A Death in the Desert – by W.R. 183

The Call to Prayer 184
In Memoriam – by Fiordelisa 185
Hope – by Fiordelisa 186
Press Onward! – by Fiordelisa 187
Cheer Up 188

POEMS FROM AMERICAN SOURCES

ST. GEORGE BEST

Al Sirat 189

J. L. M. GOUGH

The Compassionate 191

CORA WILBURN

In Defence of the Right 192
To His Imperial Majesty, Sultan Abdul Hamid II 194

GLOSSARY 197

FURTHER READING on the Liverpool Muslims 201

INTRODUCTION & ACKNOWLEDGMENTS

The poetry collected in *The Convert's Passion: An Anthology of Islamic Poetry from Late Victorian and Edwardian Britain* presents a unique insight into the mindset of late Victorian era Western converts to Islam. The complexity of the poets' lives is captured in the juxtaposition of the English language being used to extol Islam while often deriding the morals and deeds of the larger British society. Poetry was still very much a common medium of literary expression in late nineteenth century Britain as well as in Islamic cultures. Alfred Lord Tennyson's forty-year reign as England's Poet Laureate had just come to a close in 1892, and most of the luminary Islamic poets' works had been translated into English by this time. In this milieu, the British Muslim converts used poetry to express themselves and entertain their brethren.

BACKGROUND

Poetry permeates all eras of Islamic history and literature. The mainly illiterate pre-Islamic Arabs were an oral culture that used poetry to memorize the details of clan history and other facets of life deemed worthy of passing down to future generations. Poetry remained integral to the Arabs after the arrival of Islam, although poets were looked upon skeptically in the Qur'an for their braggadocio and verbal attacks on the nascent Muslim community. The Qur'an states, "And the Poets,—It is those straying in Evil, who follow them: / Seest thou not that they wander distracted in every valley?— / And that they say what they practice not?— / Except those who believe, work righteousness, engage much in the remembrance of Allah, and defend themselves only after they are unjustly attacked..."[1] Nonetheless, the prophet Muhammad himself had among his companions a preeminent Arab poet. Hassan ibn Thabit is

---

[1] Holy Qur'an (Yusuf Ali translation) 26: 224-227.

considered the first Islamic poet and he used his poems to staunchly defend the Prophet. As Islam spread, so did many Arab cultural proclivities, including a high regard for poetry.

The genesis of the publication of British Muslim poetry was the establishment of the Liverpool Moslem Society by Abdullah William Henry Quilliam in July 1887, which later became the Liverpool Moslem Institute in 1889.[2] Quilliam was a solicitor with a large practice who spent several months convalescing in Morocco in 1884. In Tangiers, he came under the influence of Hadji Abdullah, a Moroccan merchant who encouraged Quilliam to consider Islam. Upon returning to England, he spent time reading the Qu'ran and English-language materials on Islam and converted in 1885.[3] A lifelong proponent of temperance, Quilliam often spoke at the movement's meetings; after converting, he began slowly integrating Islam into his speeches. Finally, in June 1887, he affirmed that he was a Muslim after his lecture "Fanatics and Fanaticism" and within a month founded the Liverpool Moslem Society with a handful of recent converts.[4]

Initially, the group set up shop at the Vernon Temperance Hall, in Mount Vernon where Quilliam often spoke. The Muslims remained at this location for two years until they were forced to vacate by the owner. This fortuitous event led to the establishment of their permanent headquarters, the Liverpool Moslem Institute, at 8 Brougham Terrace, West Derby Road, in December 1889 with a total of 14 converts. Through the years, the Institute offered the requisite daily and Friday congregational (Jumma) Muslim prayer services, social gatherings, lectures and classes, a library, reading room, museum, a school for boys and girls, and later an orphanage (Medina Home for Children). Quilliam and his followers became internationally known after he published his work *The Faith of Islam* in 1889. Thousands of copies made their way across the Muslim world and it was translated into several eastern languages.[5] In 1890, the Liverpool Muslims were recognized and wished success by the Ottoman Sultan, Abdul Hamid II, which began a long relationship

---

[2] "A Short History of the Progress of Islam in England," *The Crescent*, January 19, 1898, pp. 35-36; "The Liverpool Moslem Institute," *The Allahbad Review*, 1890, pp. 113-115. A constitution and basic prospectus of the Institute are included.
[3] "Islam in England," *The Islamic World*, April 1894, pp. 2-3; "Quilliam, William Henry Abdullah." In *Who's Who*, 1903, p. 1128.
[4] Ibid; "A Short History of the Progress of Islam in England."
[5] Quilliam, W.H. *The Faith of Islam*. Liverpool: Willmer Bros., 1892. See, prefaces of the various editions.

between Quilliam and the court at Constantinople.[6] His budding international acclaim gave the Institute the opportunity to gain spiritual and material support from the wider Islamic World, which was keen to see Islam spread in the heart of the British Empire.

The continued expansion of contacts between the fledging British Muslims and the greater Muslim world helped set the stage for the group's most ambitious project. In 1893, *The Crescent* and *The Islamic World*, the weekly and monthly news organs of the Institute, were first published.[7] These publications were subscribed to by Muslims and non-Muslims alike across the English-speaking and Muslim worlds. As Ansari notes, "these publications were on the exchange list of around 100 foreign journals, which Quilliam regarded as 'one of the most important features of our work', since potentially it enabled the LMI [Liverpool Moslem Institute] to reach hundreds of thousands of people every week."[8] Not only did the publications garner the Liverpool Muslims widespread notoriety and broaden their international contacts, they also allowed them to share their journalistic, literary, and poetic talents. The first poems published in *The Crescent* on February 11, 1893 were authored by William Obeid-Ullah Cunliffe. The first, "Salvation Sal," was a send-up of the Salvation Army (not included in this anthology); the other, "Truth," was the first of scores of poems inspired by Islam to be published in *The Crescent* and *The Islamic World*. Poetry of all kinds would continue to be a regular feature of the periodicals until they ceased in 1908.

THE ANTHOLOGY

This anthology features more than 140 poems written by over a dozen poets. The poets' backgrounds range from amateurs inspired to write a single poem to widely published poets and writers. The most prolific poets featured in this work are Sheikh Abdullah Quilliam (50 poems) and Yehya-en-Nasr Parkinson (27 poems). Quilliam's poems cover the gamut of religious topics and human emotions, as well as odes to the Isle of Man and other esoteric personal topics. Parkinson mainly focuses on bygone eras of chivalry, particularly in Moorish Spain. His epic poems are by far the lengthiest

---

[6] "The Sultan and the Liverpool Moslems," *The Times* (London), December 20, 1890, p. 12.
[7] "A Short History of the Progress of Islam in England" and "Islam in England."
[8] Ansari, Humayun, *'The Infidel Within': Muslims in Britain since 1800*. London: Hurst & Co., 2004, p. 123.

presented in this work. Parkinson also dabbled in love poetry that often seemed a bit *risqué* for the audience of *The Crescent*. While most of the poets in the anthology are men, there are some notable women poets, including Ameenah Lincoln and Cora Wilburn.

POEM SELECTION

The poems in this anthology are mainly reproduced from *The Crescent* or *The Islamic World*, but a few come from other periodicals and monographs as noted at the end of each poem. The poems were selected on the basis of their Islamic themes, whether historical, cultural, or religious and the fact that they were written by British converts to Islam or their close associates and sympathizers in the West. However, there are some poems that do not strictly follow this rule and are included to give the reader a better sense of the complete body of work of a poet. There were dozens of poems in *The Crescent* written by native-born Muslims living in Britain or submitted from abroad, but these have not been included here. Most poems of a general nature written by non-Muslims and Muslims alike were excluded. While these poems would be of interest to many readers, they are outside the scope of this work.

EDITING POEMS

When editing the poems, the original published format was retained as much as possible, including British spelling conventions, transliterations, contractions, anachronisms, punctuation, and non-standard usage. Obvious omissions, typographical and spelling errors, and other peculiarities have been corrected whenever possible. The poets are listed alphabetically and then the poems are listed chronologically by date of publication.

BIOGRAPHIES

The brief biographies are based upon information gleaned from reviewing all available issues of *The Crescent*, the first few years of *The Islamic World*, or the original source of the poems. Otherwise, information from outside of these sources is noted in the "Other sources consulted" section immediately following the biography. Unfortunately, available biographical information is uneven, and in some cases a less prolific poet may have a more substantive biography than their more prolific colleagues. Finally, some poems were originally published under initials, pseudonyms, or anonymously. In these cases, no biographical information is available and these poems have been collocated together toward the end of the work.

ACKNOWLEDGEMENTS

My sincere thanks are extended to my daughters Imani and Anisa for their assistance in transcribing and deciphering poems, Stacy Magedanz for editing, and Michael Burgess for bringing this project to publication. I am also very grateful to Abdal Hakim Murad (Cambridge University) for his support, patience in answering my queries, and generous lending of materials.

Jazakallah khair

AHMED C(URTIS) BRANN (1870-1951)

Ahmed C. Brann was born in the Parish of Stoke Dameral, Devonport, in 1870 and baptized in the Church of England. At age eighteen he joined the military and served with the 2nd Battalion Devonshire Regiment in Rawalpindi, India (in present day Pakistan) and Upper Burma. Brann first took an interest in Islam around 1892 and at the suggestion of a local Indian Muslim began a correspondence with Sheikh Abdullah Quilliam. After being discharged in 1896, Brann returned to England and began attending the London Temporary Mosque headed by Cape Town, South Africa native, Hadjie Mahommed Dollie. Under Dollie's tutelage Brann converted to Islam in 1898. Later that year, he moved to Liverpool and joined the Liverpool Moslem Institute. Brann later became very active in the organization in 1906 and early 1907, writing several articles, leading prayers on occasion, and acting as the official Muezzin. His one poem was published in *The Crescent* in December 1906.

There Is No God but Thee

"God!—there is no God but He; the Living,
the Self-subsisting."—The Throne—Qur'an

1.

There is no God but Thee;
  No partner shares Thy Throne;
Through all, unending times and space,
  Thy Glory reigns alone
Source of all life that dwells
  In air, or land, or sea;
There is no dead or quickened thing
  But cometh, Lord, from Thee.

2.

There is no God but Thee,
  Great Ruler of the Spheres,
Thy Power created all, and still

   Sustains them through the years;
Thy Law shall rule for aye,
   Thy Justice still decree,
Thy Bounty cherish all and bring
   All bound in love to Thee.

3.

O Great, Eternal King,
O Lord of Might and Grace!
Grant that Thy servants yet may find,
With Thee, abiding place.
And hasten, Lord, the time
When mortal things shall flee,
And never-ending choirs shall sing:
   "There is no God but Thee!"

Originally published in *The Crescent*, December 12, 1906

W(ILLIAM) OBEID-ULLAH CUNLIFFE
(CA. 1831-1894)

William Obeid-Ullah Cunliffe, born circa 1831, was a resident of Brockley, London, and an engineer by trade, having been credited with designing Liverpool's noted Steble Fountain. He converted to Islam around 1892 and was an active member of the Liverpool Moslem Institute, albeit from afar, writing poems, short stories, and commentary for *The Crescent* and *The Islamic World* from 1893-94. During this period he contributed at least fifteen poems to these publications. There were likely more; however, the 1894 editions of *The Crescent* are lost to history. Upon his death, he was moved to Liverpool to be interred.

Other sources consulted:

"Facts and Events," *Latter-Day Saints' Millennial Star*, 1894, vol. 56, p. 199.

Truth

Truth, is not that which seemeth, but the thing which is,
  The mirror of the things that be, shewn in clear light.
Hold it most dear and heed thou its behests, and day, or night,
  Or shine, or shadow,—go thou, and follow it, in duty, unto bliss.

Originally published in *The Crescent*, February 11, 1893

The Orient Sun of Islam

Thousands of years hath the sun rose,
  In the glow of its Eastern hues,
Thousands of years doth the West close
  It in gloom, and in tears, of its dews.
Even so, in the Orient morning,
  Faith, true!—pure, of Allah, The One,
Rose, Earth, with its beauty, adorning,
  And sank, Westward—and darkened, its sun

O, Believers! have faith in Faith's morning,
   Know ye, Allah knoweth the best!
See, the Light of the Orient, returning
   Pure Islamic beams, o'er the West.

Originally published in *The Crescent*, April 29, 1893

Wad-El-Nejumi's Charge at Tosti[9]

Black men, and brave men, and heroes of tan,
Few men, but true men of Moslem Soudan,
Poor men, but sure men (ill fed with scant bread),
Souls, like steel of their blades, 'El-Nejumi led,
From hot desert sands, and camel-hair tent,
From bordj on the aghil, and wild jasmin's scent;
For wives, and for children, El Islam, and home,
Death-daring, death-dealing, the Soudanese come
And swoop down at Tosti, like a torrent in spray,
'Gainst the human volcano, that held them at bay:—
The steel wall of redcoats, of bullets and flame,
That swept the black patriots to death, but not shame:
By murd'rous machine guns, all mangled and torn,
With the nerve of El Islam, and heroic scorn,
O, Braves of the desert! your rude arms are nought
'Gainst the warfare that civilization hath taught
Rude scimeter, spear, shield, and hearts pulsed as one,
Few, furious, and fearless, against Christian gun,
With its vomit of death in continuous flow:
And the braves of Soudan, and of Islam fall low;
Like straws in a sand-storm, a moment wind-tossed,
Then buried, forgotten, and for ever lost.
Lost? nay, Wad-El-Nejumi's compatriots, the slain

---

[9] By "Tosti," Cunliffe means Toski (Tushkah), a town in southern Egypt. The poem describes the 1889 battle between British-led Egyptian forces and the invading Mahdist Sudanese commanded by Emir Abdur Rahman Wad-el-Nejumi. Wad-el-Nejumi was killed and the Sudanese were soundly defeated, ending the Mahdist threat to Egypt.

With their chief, yet, will rise, in their honour, again.
Who fight for their homes, kindred, right, good and faith,
Shall paradise enter:—So Allah's book saith.
Thus Wad-El-Nejumi's men died, man to man,
For faith, home, and kindred—heroes of Soudan!

   Originally published in *The Islamic World*, May 1893

The Creed of Truth

Restless dreamers of the night,
   Whose truant thought wide gropes the dark!
O, shameless souls! disclothed and stark—
   Sluggards that heed not dawn of light.

Uneasy, dream-bound on your couch,
   Ye mark no shine of Islam's sun;
Wake to its light—its truth ye vouch—
   God spake: Mahomed, God is one!

What baseless faith, though bound compact,
   With close-meshed dogmas—ropes of sand!
Faith's test is truth! not words, but fact;
   Not basic errors; truth, soul bann'd:—

No myths of ages, dark, unproved—
   Traditions crude of hidden yore;
Nor fondsome fictions, easy grooved,
   On customs lost in trackless lore.

Men's souls were formed for truth to live;
   By truth believe and serve, adore
Great Allah, Who His truth did give
   To guide aright men evermore.

Not by the monarch jewel-crowned,
   Enclothed in gold and purple state;

Not lords of earth, nor coped and gowned,
 And sacrosanct and proud prelate;

But Allah from the poor hath chose
 His messengers, to bear the truth:
The unlearned lowly who uprove
 To sow truth's seeds and tend its growth.

He called, they heard; He bade, they went;
 The God truth's taught, attesting loud.
Truth's poor apostles Allah sent—
 Scorned by the fool-wise, rich, and proud.

World's wisdom staggered, earth's saints reeled mad,
 And men and Shaitan rose, enarmed,
To crush the truth Mahomed had;
 But God's few faithful millions swarmed.

Who truth opposes wars 'gainst God;
 Untested faiths are creeds for fools;
But sure truth's faith, though mean the clod
 That bare it: meek are Allah's tools!

O, souls! be wise; to read aright
 God's holy laws, be true to truth;
From gloom dogmatic come to light
 Of God, and faith, and love, and ruth.

 Originally published in *The Islamic World*, June 1893

Sow Islam's Seed!

Hear ye, voices on the winds,
 Sounding far o'er surging seas,
For the Faithful duty finds?
 Bring ye Islam's Truth to these.
From the West come pleadful cries—

Souls are hungering for the Truth:
Eager wait, with searchful eyes,
  From dusk to dawn for Faith's renew'th
Rise, O Islam! to their needs:
  The waste West in fallow lay'th;
Sow ye now the precious seed,
  Cull the fruits of Islam's Faith.
Brethren verily are we,
  All of Islam's Holy Creed!
And the True Believer, he
  Allah's work doth, as decreed.

Originally published in *The Crescent*, June 17, 1893

The Moslimah's Jewels

In a palace of dreams, four Moslimahs slept
In peace, by the angels of Allah safe kept,
When an order of Paradise swept through the room,
And a form, veiled in light and in glory, had come,
More bright than the sun's shine, all vestured and shod,
An angel who bore them a message from God:
Arise ye, O daughters of Islam! go, bring
Me your jewels to take unto Allah, the King!
Ayeesha brought diamonds, the brightest of Ind;
And Haidee went ruddiest of rubies to find;
Khadeegeh her riches of rare pearls, too, brought;
But the other came, trembling and weeping, with nought.
The angel's eyes seemed to glance through her a fire,
And his sword, like the lightning, seemed flashing entire,
As she sank in dumb terror, abashed, at his feet,
For pity and mercy, so precious and sweet.
Said the angel: "Speak! where are the gems thou didst have?"
Said the woman: "I sold them; the money I gave."
"Thou hast sold them, saidst thou? and, the price gavest to whom?"
"To the foodless and poor, and to poor Hajees, some;
Nor evil I meant it, nor deemed it to be;

May Allah's compassion show mercy to me!"
She sobbed, faint and fearful, nor dared her eyes raise
For dread of his holy and soul-searching gaze.
At length she looked up. The angel was gone;
And, clad in pure vesture, she knelt there alone;
And the sweetness of Paradise shone on her face
With the beauty of houris, and angelic grace;
And the best of all jewels, from Allah, she had
On the vesture of angels, in which she was clad.
And Zee'neb's pure soul had met, painless, Death's kiss,
And entered abode in the gardens of bliss.

Originally published in *The Islamic World*, July 1893

The Hajee

An Allegory

Out of the West to Eastern light
   Forth came a man, nor he, be-dight
With trappings rich, nor charger rode;
   But, sore atrudge on foot, he strode;
Nor lance, nor deathly match-lock bore,
   Nor scimeter, to stain in gore;
But held in hand a papyrus roll,
   No virgin page, but scripted scroll,
Which, half unope'd he paced and read,
   Or, pondering, paused and stopped his tread,
Through desert sands, by rock bound pass,
   Beneath sun blaze and sky of brass,
Whose fiery ardours havoc wrought
   On verdure, still he tramped, and sought
The hand from whence the scroll was brought,
   The strange—the new, wise lore it taught:
The school of truth,—Great Allah's lore;
   And eastward sought its source,—foot-sore.
At length he reached that Orient land,

The Kaabah's walls he wist, and scanned,
And spake, a passer in the street,
  A Moslem beggar, he did meet,—
"Allah is One!—I know, and this,—
  "Mohammed; his apostle is;
"Truth!—God's Koran is, too, forsooth;
  "Teach me El-Islam's other truth?"

"Allah is God!—and other,—none!"
  The beggar said,—"Faith, truth,—are one!
"Obey the truth; then thou hast done;"
  "To Paradise doth go, such one."

London, July 18th, 1893

Originally published in *The Moslem World,* August 1893

Sands

Idly maudling, crouched a boy,
  Counting, casting grains of sand,
Shaped, in grains, a fashioned toy,
  Clutched a heap in tight-closed hand.

Tossed the handful, and 'twas gone—
  Picked and gathered, grain by grain,
Persevering slowly on,
  Soon to cast them down again.

Then an image he essayed;
  But, anon, it crumbled down.
Then, a palace of sands made—
  Roof, walls, turrets, tumbled down.

Once again he counted out
  Grains, to call them golden grain;
Moulds a crown—all comes to nought—

Palace, crown, and hoard, in vain.

Said a grey-beard to the youth,
  "So man wasteth time and pains,
Toying with Life's sands, while truth
  Lies hid in't in golden grains."

Wealth, beyond all golden hoard;
  Truth of truth, for evermore;
Truth of Allah's Holy Word!
  Wisdom from Al-Koran's store!

Originally published in *The Crescent*, September 30, 1893

The Dawn of Faith

Before me lay, unread, the Book of Truth,
And priest-wove creeds bound blind mine eyes from youth;
The sun-lit day ebbed drowsily to night;
God sent His angel to unseal my sight.

Then, lo, His marvelous pages seemed to rise
In jeweled words, that lighted heart and eyes;
And sun, and world, and stars, and crescent shone;
I read the page, and saw writ, "God is One!"

I saw the flocks and herds, all living things of earth,
Peoples and nations, of all climes and birth—
The mighty things of Nature He hath done,
And all things bowed, attesting "God is One!"

And grass, and herb, and tree, and flower of field,
And corn, and fruit—the alms of God—revealed,
With all the starry firmament a yon,
The truth—God's truth of truths—that "God is One!"

I winged o'er ocean, searched its trackless waves,
Where the dead lie, unwrecked, in storm-laved graves;
Where Allah's creatures sport in myriad forms;
"Lo, God is One!" soft whispered the stilled storms.

I saw through cloven heavens the lightning's crash;
"Lo, God is One!" blazed the electric flash;
The deafening echoes shook the shuddering skies;
"Lo, God is One!" the deep-voiced thunder cries.

I cried, "Great Allah! what is man to Thee?"
"Read thou, and learn the truth, and serve thou Me!"
This was the answer to my heart of dearth;
I bowed, adoring, with my face to earth.

Originally published in *The Islamic World*, November 1893

A Moslem's Prayer

Al Bari!—Master of us all,
Low we, in adoration, fall
Before Thee, Allah!—Greatest, Best!
We are Thy creatures: each Thy guest.
In the vast universe Thou'st made,
From suns, and worlds, to grassy blade,
Thou dost what Thou will'st; 'tis best;
For all Thy creatures Thou hast blest.
Thine only be all praise and prayer,
All works of good and actions fair,
Alone are Thine; Who doth prepare
The path, the will, the means to do
The thing which Thou hast called us to.

Praise be to Thee!—for praise is Thine!
Prayers be to Thee! Allah, incline
Thine aid to us; for it we need
In impulse to each righteous deed.

Guide us aright, and by Thy power
Help us in good or evil hour
To do Thy will, and so abide
Thy servants alway, what betide:
For Thou art God—Allah, alone—
God, All-Creator!—God, the One!
Who, by Mohammed, spake us, thus:
Peace be upon him, and on us!

   Originally published in *The Moslem World*, November 1893

The Alms of Aziz

Said Aziz, "Verily, God is good!
I have more than sufficient for warmth and food.
Having health and comfort, what need of more?
I will give in alms—deeds the surplus—o'er."

Then he stood and divided his wealth in three,
"This is for alms to the poor," said he,
"This for poor strangers and hajees be,
And this for faiths spread beyond the sea!"

Then he paused and pondered, counting the same—.
"Bismillah! who knows what fate may come?
I will wait and put aside this store
For a time, and make it a little more."

So he gathered again each golden pile,
And hoarded them up in his coffers awhile;
Until one thought more sprang into his head:
"I will put it to use and to profit," he said.

And one part at interest high he lent,
Another for trades, in merchandise spent;
The portion remaining, he pondered about,
"Shall I keep or invest it?" he questioning thought.

"I think I will keep it to give to the poor,
In alms, one by one, as they come to my door."
So the third and last portion he put it away,
To be used in alms gifts on some other day.

That night to his hoard the robbers crept,
And took it away while Aziz slept;
The next day his merchandise vanished in fire,
Converted to ashes, down-trodden in mire.

There remained yet the loan, out at highest per cent,
But the borrower ran off, the loan with him went.
"Alas! for the alms-deeds undone," Aziz cried,
Then Aziz fell sick, wept, impoverished, and died.

   Originally published in *The Islamic World*, December 1893

Ibrahim's Sin

Hassan and Omer went to pray
At the holy Mosque ere break of day.
Omer prayed, and soon had done,
But Hassan prayed, and prayed long on,
Ere sunrise to the set of sun.
And while the night's dark hours did run,
And yet prayed he from morn to night,
And from its fall to dawn of light.
And scarcely stayed to pause or eat,
But prayer on prayer he did repeat.
Ibrahim saw it, and, said he,
"Bismillah! What is this we see?
One prays too long and one too short—
The right prayer is another sort."
And said his prayers and went his way,
Thinking of Hassan all the day.
At nightfall, ere he went to rest,

A wandering beggar came as guest,
Whom Ibrahim tended, washed his sores,
And gave him best of all his stores;
And while he for his guest did care,
He spake of Hassan's and Omer's prayer.
Then, "Allah bless thee, brother abide
Thou on my couch, rest by my side."
They slept. At Isha Ibrahim arose,
But where his guest is, not he knows.
Yet when his Isha prayer was done,
There guest stood, radiant as the sun.
"Doubter of good in other's deed,"
Said he, "How knowest thou the needs?
Know thou it was to conquer self,
That Hassan prayed for his soul's health,
And Omer's Namaz soon was through,
For work that Allah willed him do."
Then Ibrahim low in sorrow bowed,
For thought of evil, and wept loud—
"Allah, compassionate," cried he, "Wise,
Alas! mine evil heart and eyes—
Alas! for me, and all the wrong
I wrought by evil thought and tongue.
Forgive my sin, and make me wise,
Oh, Allah!" said the guest, "Arise,
Look on the book I hold, and read,
And learn the virtue of a deed;
Herein are penned, excepting nought,
The good and ill which thou hast wrought."
He read a sin crossed "Good intent,"
Another crossed "He did repent;"
A good deed marked with "Evil thought,"
And one marked "Good, though nothing wrought,"
One "Hypocrite in holy guise;"
One "Angel, feasted, beggar, wise."
And new light fell on Ibrahim's eyes.

The guest said, "Go, now, and be wise!"

Originally published in *The Islamic World*, December 1893

The Enchanted Fallen

 An Allegory of Life

I wandered awide by the racing tide,
Through a green and sunny valley,
With the dancing beam played the smiling stream,
 While it laughed out musically,
 And the euphonies of glad bird throats
  With the scented breezes dally.
 Oh! music and shine, made seem so divine,
  That valley so happy and sunny.

The bright-plumed birds, in their radiant bowers,
Vied with the many-hued glist of the flowers,
With the thousand sweet odours that winged on the breeze;
And the leaf-woven thatch of the verdured trees,
 Bent low with the ripe fruit laden,
 In the groves of that beautiful Aiden.
 And the glades of that gladsome Aiden.

 Yet I wished not to tarry, I willed not to stay,
  On the beautiful banks of youth's river—
 Plucked I nectarine fruit and wandered away,
  And believed 'twould continue for ever.

The music, and sheen, and sweet scented bowers,
The iridescent plumage of bright birds and flowers,
 Oh! I thought they would terminate never.
The delectable fruits that the verdure did grow,
With the glist, and the glow, and the fair river's flow,
With the ever-green glades and the golden sunshine,
The odours of Aiden and pleasance divine,

Ah! I deemed they would last, aye, and ever.

Yet I wandered aside, now stilly, now wide,
And now grew tumultuous and narrow the tide.
The flowers were all faded, the gay birds had flown,
And the leaves, sere and yellow, the stark glades had strewn;
No musical murmur re-echoed the air,
And but skeleton boughs were left, bony and bare,
   Like spectres to haunt the lone river,
   Like ghosts on that once happy river.

Where the surly blasts shriek, or low mutter despair,
And through grey rime, goes weeping, with wailing and blare,
In fretful disquiet and fitful despair,
   On the banks of that unhappy river;
That ever on floweth more madly and grows
More darksome and dismal, whilst over it close.

And around us, and behind us, while onward we fly,
Huge barriers, enshadowed with gaunt misery,
And ensentinelled ever by grim, ghostly fears,
That appal us, and hold us in terrors and tears;
In this valley of shadows, the shadows of tombs,
Where the murmur of death, or the sobbing wind comes.

Which howleth, and moaneth, and muttereth despair,
That in agony creeps on the shuddering air;
And we weep o'er joys wasted and unfruitful flowers,
O'er precious wealth wasted, of life's precious hours;
While, louder, up cometh, and nearer the roar
Of the tide of life, leaping the brink of death o'er,
To the dark, dismal chasm, the abyss, "Evermore."

But, lo! from the heavens there beameth a star,
One lamp in the gloom, around, near, and afar;
And a rift in the clouds, lined with silver, is drawn;
And a golden curved horn from the river-gloom shown;

And, broader and brighter, the argent rim shows,
And star upon star, unveiled, heavens disclose.

Until skies are aglow, lit with splendour and light,
And the crescent shines peacefully forth, pure and bright.
As a bride in her beauty and innocent sweet.
When she riseth, unveiled, her loved one to meet.
So, unto Earth's outcast truth-seeker, 'mid tears,
Sorrow, gloom—with peace, beautiful Islam appears.

As the moon reflex light, of the sun casts abroad,
Doth the crescent, Islam, reflect truth-rays of God;
And the light of pure faith beams from Orient skies,
On the dense clouded West, where the faith-fallen lies;
And the desert of Araby hath borne us a flower,
Which the fragrance of Paradise scatters earth o'er.

And where'er in the wild wastes its seed taketh root,
It groweth, and bloometh, and beareth fair fruit,
In the beauty of holiness, under fair skies,
While its odours in prayer unto Allah doth rise,
And sweet food for Earth's famished ones its fruit doth afford,
The feast of pure faith, truth of God's holy word.

Originally published in *The Islamic World*, January 1894

The Thief, Old Time[10]

Old time is a common thief,
   And hoarding of gain is madness,
He steals our hours, maketh life but brief,
   Purloins our youth, filches away its gladness;
He wiles unto indulgence men's belief,
   Then robs the pleasure, and we wake to sadness,
And vanished hours but leave us pangs of grief.

---

[10] This poem was written a week prior to Cunliffe's death.

O time! hoary Old rogue, thou
   Who slyly encompasseth us to borrow
Life's treasures—of its toy, in vogue now—
   And, minus luxury or joy, in sorrow
Leaves us, or kicks us, like a dog, low,
   Whining and yelping for a better morrow,
When lust fails, and life clogs low,
   Robbed, beaten, kicked by Time, carrion, into Death's furrow.
     So men lie, so men die,
     Waiting still, good or ill,
     Whining, begging, praying, trusting—
     At the end of all the evil done, and lusting—
     For salvation, and a blissful morrow:
     For to enter Paradise, and leave all sorrow;
     Pleading, tearful, eager, with last breath, for pity,
     Murderers, for greed and lust, in city,
     They who took, and kept, that Allah gave to others,
     Oppressors of the widow and the orphan, and their poor
        afflicted bothers:
Who in all sin, and evil thing, and beastly lust, did wallow,
Cry they piteously for mercy unto compassionate Allah!
Though never an honest prayer, or goodly deed, was there,
Their hand, or heart, or lip, before, to hallow.
     Late!—late is the prayer, never before a care;
     Comes repentance this of fear?—guilty despair?
     Say, how will such soul fare?—Is it prayer?
     Is there hope for such of Just, Avenging Allah?

Originally published in *The Islamic World*, May 1894

Life![11]

Golden childhood's happy day,
Toying, glides in smiles away,
Like a slumber, like a song

---

[11] This poem was written a few days prior to Cunliffe's death.

Of glad music from sweet tongue.
Youth, then, passeth careless on,
Prone to mischief, sport and fun;—
Laughing, loitering life away,
Recks no learning, loveth play.

Rising fast to adult hours,
Hope, in dreaming fancy, towers;
Gilded pleasures charm our eyes;
Fond ambitions luring rise.
Plodding, planning matured age,
Thoughtful, useful, toil doth wage;
Work for rightful purpose sought.
And the end is duly wrought.

Eager, scheming, middle life,
Greater gains now makes its strife;
Careful, stinting, seeks to save,
And competent means to have.
Later years, penurious flow;
Pinching abstinence comes now,
Scraping, hoarding avarice rules,
Mean and spare to enrich fools.

Old age shuffles on apace,
Weary, flaggeth in the race,
Weak and fainting, slacks and stays,
Sad, repentant, weeps and prays.
Such is the mean of human life;
Such,—man's common course and strife:
Men die the victims of their greed,
Nor Allah, nor example, heed.

As insects, liquid honey in
They sip, sink, perish in their sin;
Like flies they buzz and beat the air,
The flower and viscid sweets their care.

Eager to satiate desire,
They gluttonous dash, stay stuck, expire,
Defunct, they noisome taint the air,
And souls are doomed to hell's despair.

Originally published in *The Islamic World*, June 1894

VALFRID "FRIIDI" HEDMAN (1872-1939)

A native of Tavastehus, Finland, (Elias Johan) Valfrid Hedman had a long career translating Finnish literature and poetry to English. He also composed poetry in both languages. Hedman had a deep interest in India and Indian religions and appears to have converted to Islam during his correspondence with Sheikh Abdullah Quilliam beginning in 1899. He was a relatively frequent contributor of poems and articles to *The Crescent* from 1900-03 and then again from 1906-08. Hedman also translated works in Scandinavian and other languages for republication in *The Crescent* and *The Islamic World*. Over the years, he also had poetry published in popular periodicals such as *Notes and Queries*.

The Sisterhood of Languages

My fragrant Finnish, soft and sweet!
   Thou art my mother dear!
In every rumour thee I meet,
   In deepest silence hear.

Thy song has lulled my childhood's sleep,
   In Finnish soughed our firs,
Thou gav'st me joy, thou mad'st me weep,
   Thy voice me charms and stirs.

To steel-clad Swedish, full of force,
   A cherished sister brave,
I also bring a toast, of course;
   To all Norse kindred wave.

First to that Danish damsel, and
   To fair Norwegian bold,
Advancing to the Eddas' land,
   Where tales of old are told.

Great English, mighty, glorious, and
   With bold, majestic mien,
Invincible her sceptred hand
   She lifts, my homaged Queen!

She is the Empress of the World,
   Her power never wanes,
Her colours proudly are unfurled,
   In every clime she reigns.

Her mother was of Woden's kin,
   Old Anglo-Saxon, though
Much Roman blood the child sucked in,
   Which in her veins does flow.

She learned is. To her there be
   No Western lore unknown,
Old India's secrets studied she,
   All seeds of knowledge sown.

But from an olden Celtic wood
   A challenge now I hear,
Strange accents, little understood,
   Welsh whispers in my ear.

Hail, German! of Teutonic birth
   The blue-eyed splendid maid,
With rosy cheeks, but iron-girth,
   Thy laurels shall not fade.

Of one branch of Germanic breed
   I still shall sing the fames;
In noble chain a precious bead,
   E'en Dutch has got her claims.

The tongue that Roman eagles brought
   To regions distant, far,

Has justly mine attention caught,
   Pure, brave its accents are.

'Tis Latin. To her daughters flees
   My thought enraptured—all
Of ancient blood new offspring these
   In Speech's banquet-hall.

A celebrated charming flirt
   Of studied manners, bright,
Is French; her waist is flower-girt,
   She's stylish and polite.

But that's not all. She talent shows,
   Is educated well,
Loved, envied, by her friends, her foes;
   Who could her suitors tell?

Italian is of this great race
   The supplest spruce, sublime;
In smiles does wreathe her gentle face,
   Her song has graceful chime.

And Spain is a lady fine,
   Black hair of velvet shade,
Two continents she does combine,
   Her charms are well displayed.

I may now mention Portuguese
   Refined, far-reached, deft;
Then opposite my fancy flees
   To Catalonian left.

In the enamored minstrel's speech
   A tune, Provençal, fair.
Then, parting, of the Danube reach
   The banks, Roumanian there.

Hungarian, she is proud, you know,
   And can afford to be;
I celebrate her youthful glow,
   Her vigour, and her glee.

To noble Greek, on classic ground,
   Both ancient and the new,
Whose forehead lingers olive-crowned,
   My compliments are due.

Melodious Polish well a kiss
   Deserves; and in her strife,
I swear to this maltreated "miss"
   Prosperity and life.

Armenian, too, how do you do?
   And wild Albanian then?
To these I must now bid adieu,
   But hope to meet again.

Abundant Arabic divine
   As goddess worship I.
The desert's daughter's leonine,
   Pure, sanguine blood flush high!

Her tunes have once illumed the world,
   Her accents risen high,
The Crescent's banners she unfurled
   In region far and nigh.

Here of her Hebrew cousin now
   I find a chance to think,
Before this "rose of Sharon" bow,
   And tie another link.

Of other kindred still be told
   Amharic and Tigré,
Twin-daughters of Ethiopic old;
   Now Syriac shares my play.

Thee, musing Persian, I adore,
   Fine jasmine-bosomed fay;
When listening to thy listful lore
   In ecstasy I lay.

In Brahma's land now Hindee, wide,
   And Hindostanee bloom,
The other Aryan sisters bide,
   More veiled and hidden lome.

There budding 'neath her sunny skies,
   I Gujaratee see;
Marathee lithe, in native guise,
   A welcome hails to me.

And on the holy Ganges' banks
   Bengalee do I meet;
Her rivers five Punjabee flanks
   That intersect her seat.

For dear old mother Sanscrit's sake
   A while I beg to stop,
My dutiful obeisance make,
   An ancient garland drop.

What shall I say of Singhalese
   Imbedded in her home,
The mythful isle that stormy seas
   Encircle with their foam?

Dravidian tribes I visit next,
   To Deccan wend my way,

My wishes best, blushed and perplexed,
   To Tamil there I say.

Down to Malay my fancy flees;
   The equatorial line
It crosses, and to Javanese
   Reach aspirations mine.

Monosyllabic accents strike
   My ears, and Annamese,
Burmese, and Siamese alike,
   Thus, in their turn, I seize.

Behind the Himalayas high,
   Snow-mantled, glorious, grand,
Wise Tibetan has caught my eye
   In "the forbidden land."

The islands of the rising sun
   Far in the farthest East
I saw, and Japanese I won,
   She is none of the least.

Born of Osman's great noble stems,
   With Persian flowers stuck,
Embellished with Arabian gems
   With utmost skill and luck,

Well-sounding Turkish I bring last,
   She is my darling bride,
With her my lots of life I cast—
   May Allah be our guide.

   Originally published in *The Crescent*, January 8, 1902

The Muslim's Heaven

In the shade of green bowers
   Fresh fountains are springing,
Grow sweet scented flowers,
   And bulbuls are singing.

The houris, the black-eyed,
   So perfect in beauty,
A welcome do whisper,
   Now pleasure is duty.

Sweet wines there are flowing
   In rivers and fountains,
Cool breezes are blowing
   So balmy from mountains.

   Originally published in *The Crescent*, June 24, 1903

To the Materialistic Christian

Thou keepest Christmas, and dost it fully,
With food and drinking, all—beautifully,
At table sitting with knife and fork,
Thy stomach filling with dirty pork.

   Originally published in *The Crescent*, December 23, 1903

Stray Lines

She plays the pauses perfectly,
   And dissonances due,
It's all a sweet disharmony,
   Discordance full and true.

Conservatives, they say, are those
   That hate the thing that's new,

So do the dogs, they are, I guess,
   Conservatives not true.

To polygamy the Western maid
   Objects with horror due,
She doesn't want it openly—
   Although she knows 'tis true.

   Originally published in *The Crescent*, January 6, 1904

The Rose of Sharon

Oh, daughter of Zion, of dark complexion,
Who, 'midst a nation so pale and chilly,
Go'st proud and noble, a black-eyed beauty,
To them art near, and yet a stranger.

Those dreaming eyes do not them cherish,
Their fire betokens the lands of fable,
And for the Orient thy heart is throbbing,
And for it only thy fine lip smiling.

Thou, rose of Sharon, white-hued yet somber!
Far, far hast roamed from thy native country,
But ever keptst thou her ancient customs,
The faith of fathers, so pure and holy.

And e'en the language—oh, would it were
That thou hadst kept it in practice also!
Does it revive? Will yet in Hebrew
The tunes arise from the harp of David?

   Originally published in *The Crescent*, June 1, 1904

The Nirvana

On the rising banks of the Ganges great,
   The cradle of India wide,
Does a Brahmin stand and meditate,
   For Nirvana his soul has sighed.

But only the pure its bosom reach,
   Oblivion for them is due.
The "Karma": thoughts, actions and passions teach
   Our lives to begin anew.

Yet far in the distance is looming the land
   Of eternal emptiness or
Of eternal bliss—as you understand
   The charms of that dusk-dimmed shore.

Originally published in *The Crescent*, July 20, 1904

HENRI MUSTAPHA LÉON

Henri Mustapha Léon was a medical doctor from Paris. He was an active member of the Liverpool Moslem Institute from 1899-1908, attending events, giving lectures, making donations, and writing articles and poems for *The Crescent* and *The Islamic World*. In 1900, he was named as an Honorary Physician to the Medina House for Children, the Institute's orphanage, as well as Honorary Secretary in 1903 and 1907. Léon also taught French and Arabic at the Liverpool Muslim College in 1902. In 1905, along with other longstanding members, he was presented with an official seal of the Institute. Léon was a member and officer of the Ancient Order of Zuzimites, a fraternal organization to which many of the Liverpool Muslims belonged. It has been suggested by some scholars that Léon is simply a pseudonym of Sheikh Abdullah Quilliam. However, institute and independent press reports of dozens of events at the Institute show that both men were present on many occasions from 1899-1908. There is evidence that the Sheik used the pseudonym Haroun Mustapha Léon and sometimes variations on Henri M. Léon, but this did not occur until a decade after Léon's active period with the Institute.

Victoria[12]

   In Memoriam

Sweet mother! gracious ruler of the nation,
   The sands of life at last have run away,
And thou, dear soul, hast passed beyond the border
   Unto the dawn of an eternal day.

Not dawn it is, for in the life eternal
   All human time divisions cease to be,
And there is nought but everlasting glory
   And sweet communion 'twixt thy God and thee.

---

[12] This poem was written on the occasion of Queen Victoria's death.

Full sixty years and more have sped since that glad day
   When thou wast crowned, a maiden fair and sweet;
But now thy gracious reign has drawn unto its close,
   And the world weeps in sorrow at thy feet.

Victoria!—that name of deathless memory—
   Thy fame will e'er resound throughout the land;
Good, gracious, kind and merciful to all,
   A sweet and worthy member of the heavenly band.

So must all human things attain their end;
   But it is hard to lose thee, when so long
Thy name has been a household god to us,
   A word to conjure with in deed and song.

Dear Queen! a hard and troubled life was thine,
   But thy sweet nature conquered every pain;
And through the stress of sadness and of sorrow
   Thy smile broke out like sunshine after rain.

This is our prayer upon the earth beneath:
   That thou, in thy bright mansion up above,
Wilt find thy earthly consort throned there,
   And taste through time the bliss of heavenly love.

   Originally published in *The Crescent*, January 30, 1901

The Two Foes

In a great war for consecrated ground,
One who loved Christ, and one who served Mahound,
Encountered manly, so that Christian knight
And zealous Moslem fell in that fierce fight.

And, since so wildly they had waged the strife,
Their anger scarce could pass with passing life.
O'er their pale corpses hung their souls yet wroth:

Till a strong angel bent and raised them both.

"What," shrieked the Christian, "would'st thou bear my foe?"
"In angel's arms shall a cursed Muslim go?"
Cried the proud knight. The radiant angel bent
His stately head to hush their discontent.

"Know ye, bewildered souls," he softly said,
"All those who bravely battled, being dead,
Praise God alike in one angelic host,
Who, to serve truth, have counted life well lost.
For men, 'midst whirling clouds of smoke and flame,
God's shadow dimly see, and give it name:
Some on Jehovah call, on Allah some,
And some fight bravely, though their lips be dumb.
Learn, faithful spirits, when the strife waxed hot,

For the same God ye fought, yet knew it not:
And, now the pangs of death are overpast,
The same wide heaven shall hold ye both at last."

Originally published in *The Crescent*, April 27, 1904

AMEENAH (EMILY) LINCOLN

Ameenah Lincoln began a correspondence with Sheikh Abdullah Quilliam in 1902 while at New Brighton, England, and spent that summer with the Liverpool Muslims attending events and contributing at least one paper for presentation. It is unclear when Lincoln converted to Islam, but she had apparently spent a considerable amount of time living in India during the late 1890s. In 1904 she again lived among the Liverpool Muslims before sailing for Bombay in November of that year. Most of her poems were published in *The Crescent* in the middle of 1904, although many of them were written several years earlier.

Other sources consulted:

> Murad, Abdal Hakim. *Muslim Songs of the British Isles*. London: Quilliam Press, 2005.

La Illa Ha, Illa Allah!

This glorious proclamation
  Th' Arabian Prophet gave,
A fiat to his nation
  And freedom to the slave,
    La illa ha, illa Allah!
As far as it can go,
  Proclaims One God,
  On sea and sod,
As countless millions shew.

Now, God's name be exalted
  To earth's remotest bound,
These words nor stay'd, nor halted,
  And ever shall resound,
    La illa ha, illa Allah!
In peace or war declare
  They'll bless home life,

   And in the strife
They Islam's foes shall scare.

Muhammed's holy work complete
   Revivified the East,
He was the promis'd Paraclete,
   Prophet, King and Priest
Let every tongue this truth declare,
   And every life attest,
There's but one God, He has no peer,
   Till from North, South and West
     La illa ha, illa Allah!
Shall sound o'er land and sea,
   This universal creed shall show
God's power and unity.

   Originally published in *The Crescent*, October 22, 1902

Hope Delusive!

Hope is merely expectation,
   The baseless pile an idiot rears,
Soon his fanciful creation
   Is swept away in floods of tears

'Tis like a blossom-laden tree
Which fruit shall never bear,
   Its promise to futurity,
   Pledg'd in flow'rets fair,
Is broken, and those flow'rets fall,
Of thy dead hopes the fun'ral pall

And as the desert pilgrim sees
   The mirage which his bosom cheers,
The cooling stream beneath the trees,
   As he approaches, disappears

Hope's emblems these, they serve to show
All is delusive here below,
   But, if unerring our prevision,
   Above fond hopes will find fruition
There God will grant the crown and palm,
To Faithful followers of Islam

Originally published in *The Crescent*, December 16, 1903

Indian Trees

A psalm for the palm, the Oriental palm
   That adorns the hills and plains,
Tho' lightnings play o'er the Himalay
   It defies the storms and the rains.
Its crest it rears thro' the icy spears
   Of the Suleimani range,
Tho' cycles come and go in that home of the snow,
   Its genus knows not change.

A hymn for the pine, for the aromatic pine,
   With its blessed healing pow'r,
Its pungent scent is a medicament,
   A boon to the rich and poor.

The aloe is blest in the East and West,
   Of patience it is the type;
For it takes a hundred years ere its blossom appears
   In beauty full and ripe.

Thro' all Hindustan the holy banian
   The Hindus venerate;
Its boughs immense, like Vishnu's beneficence,
   Their devotions stimulate.

And now I'll raise a paean of praise
   To the sacred pie-pul tree;

Beneath its spreading boughs the gentle Hindu bows
   To his unknown deity.

And who dares jeer at his homage sincere
   When he prostrates on the sod?
'Tis truer and safer than to worship a wafer
   As the flesh and blood of God.

May 9th

   Originally published in *The Crescent*, May 18, 1904

The Suleiman Stone (The Opal)[13]

El Hajar Suleimani
A Legend of Muree, in the Himalayas

O'er the Himalayas King Solomon strode
To seek the Sahaen Queen's abode,
On the highest peak he laid his hand,
And sprang to Arabia's burning sand.
Beneath that peak, in the gloomy mine,
For ages had slept the opaline;
Known till then by its ghastly hue
Of a dead-fish eye, white and blue;
It had ever borne an evil fame,
And brought its bearer sorrow and shame.
But at King Solomon's touch, behold,
The shim'ring gem was streak'd with gold!
Thenceforth the baneful opaline
Was with qualities benign
Endow'd; who wears it on her breast
Is now with truth and wisdom blest,
But thro' the earth these mines alone

---

[13] The Suleiman Stone is fabled for having powers of protection in Eastern religions.

Guard the fateful Solomon stone.

Peshawur, December 5, 1900

Originally published in *The Crescent*, June 8, 1904

The Palm Tree on the Dublin Mountains at Newbrook, Rathfarnham[14]

In the Emerald Isle, on a mountain side,
   There grew a stately palm.
I saw it in its towering pride,
   And I said, "Oh friend, salaam!
How came you to this climate cold
   Where the sun is seldom seen?
Do you miss his refulgent rays of gold
   When our winds blow sharp and keen?

"Do you miss your kin in the East afar.
   The pine and the peepal tree,
The shesham and the deader,
   The gandel and mulberee?
An alien I was once like you
   In India's glowing land,
Where the moonbeams of electric blue
   Sear the brain like a brand."

   The Palm's Reply:—
"I came from cloud capp'd Himalay,
   The home of eternal snow;
I was rooted here in Iran's clay
   One hundred years ago.

---

[14] Rathfarnham is a suburb of Dublin, where Newbrook House is situated and likely the estate Lincoln is describing.

"Here are no storms, the genial wind
   Blows round me fresh and free;
And Newbrook's master is good and kind,
   And proud of his dear palm tree.
So I have taken the trees around
   To be my kith and kin,
Their origin, like mine, is found
   The Eastern pale within."

That night, a fearful tempest rose,
   As if by Afreets led,
It smote the palm repeated blows,
   And in the morn 'twas dead!
Now, Newbrook's master mourns the palm,
   Its beauty he'll ne'er forget.
And I for it now write this psalm
   To testify regret.

   Originally published in *The Crescent*, July 13, 1904

The Fort Agra![15]

This famous Fort! this noble citadel,
Evok'd the past as by th' enchanter's spell,
Here the great Mougol Potentates held sway,
And came to end inglorious in our day
Baber, the mighty King, and kingly man,
And of his line Akbar and Shah Jehan,
His palace here, his chamber of repose
Fill'd with the scent of lime, and orange trees,
Panel'd with sacred Modya flower and rose
In varied hues, and dainty traceries,
The roof is conical, on eight shafts rear'd,
And arabesqued in every brilliant hue,

---

[15] This poem recounts the well known Mughal rulers who governed from the Agra Fort in India during the sixteenth to seventeenth centuries.

Arches, thro' which the glowing dawn appear'd
Pencil'd with crimson, gold, and azure blue
Balconies, and balustrade,
Pierc'd, and carved with curious taste,
Pillars, and lofty architrave
With precious stones inlaid, and trac'd,
Porphyry, and cornelian red,
Sapphires, and lapis lazuli
Adorn'd the Sultan's costly bed,
And vied with sleep to charm the eye,
Whilst round the chissel'd cornice ran
The noble texts of Alkoran!
Shah Jehan's was a dreadful fate!
Not far from this luxurious room
Where he had dwelt in royal state,
He languished in a living tomb,
For seven long, and weary years
Within a little Mosque confin'd,
He was to solitude, and tears,
Condemn'd by Aurungzebe! Here blind,
He asked that he some youths might teach
To balance his half-crazy mind
He was refus'd, no human speech
Might his condition mitigate,
The Jumna 'neath his prison wall
Roll'd, where he had rear'd to Noor-Mahal
The costly shrine. Now, blind and old,
He doth his liberation wait
His bitter memories can't be told,
Or how he mourn'd his cruel fate,
Waiting for Azrael's call
To meet again his Noor Mahal!

Agra, February 1899

  Originally published in *The Crescent*, January 17, 1906

YEHYA-EN-NASR (JOHN) PARKINSON (1874-1918)

Yehya-en-Nasr Parkinson was born in Kilwinning, Scotland, to parents of Irish descent in 1874. Raised by his grandparents, he received a boarding school education until about age thirteen when his grandparents became ill. He later studied several areas of science, but took especially keen interest in astronomy and had several articles on the subject published. Parkinson studied philosophy and religion, joining the United Presbyterian Church. He soon broke away, began studying Islam, and converted in short order. Initially, he wrote articles for *The Crescent* under the pseudonym Ingomar, including the serialized work "The Sword of Islam" in 1901. He then used his given and Muslim name on dozens of poems and articles from 1901-08. Parkinson was as active as possible with the Liverpool Muslims, but remained a resident of Scotland and Ireland, only occasionally attending events and lecturing in Liverpool. In 1905, he received the decoration of the Imperial Order of Medjideh from the Turkish Sultan for his poetry. That same year, he was elected one of several vice-presidents of the British Muslim Association. Along with many members of the Liverpool Muslims, he actively participated and served as an officer in the fraternal group the Ancient Order of Zuzimites. Parkinson was second only to Sheikh Abdullah Quilliam in the quantity of poetry published in *The Crescent* and *The Islamic World*. His poems appeared from 1901-07. In 1908, he moved to Rangoon, Burma, where he published the works *Essays on Islamic Philosophy* and *Muslim Chivalry* in 1909.

Other sources consulted:

"John Yehya-En-Nasr Parkinson, F.S.G.," *The Islamic Review*, February 1914, vol. 2, no. 2, pp. 64-65.

Parkinson, J. Yehya-en-Nasr. *Essays on Islamic Philosophy*. Rangoon: British Burma Press, 1909.

Zengi[16]

The sword you gaze upon my child,
   Thine eyes with eager passion scan;
Has flashed amid the tempest wild,
   Where Zengi led the Muslim van;
The jewelled hilt whose rays of fire
   Might scorn the glory of the sun,
The tempered blade whose touch of ire
   Made streams of deepest crimson run;
Unmatched on many a field of fight,
   But dimmed in many a battle won;
It made and unmade many a knight,
   For it was Zengi's own, my son.
Methinks I see his streaming crest,
   Like snow-white foam upon the wave,
Where'er the thronging squadrons prest,
   Amid the bravest of the brave.
Listen! and I will tell you, lad,
   The story of a soldier true.
No abler chief for combat clad,
   Nor better brand in danger drew;
When but a youth of fourteen years
   Sages revered his comely form.
He led his father's cavaliers
   In summer calm and winter storm;
His early days foretold renown,
   Predestined by the hand of fate,
Princes upheld his youthful crown
   Until he grew to man's estate.
It was a time of bitter strife,
   Of broiling day and night alarms,

---

[16] The subject of this poem is Imad al-Din Zangi (1087-1146), the Turkish founder of the Zangid dynasty of northern Iraq and Syria. He was the first Muslim commander to successfully lead counter-Crusade campaigns. The poem also describes his assassination.

Murder and plunder both were rife,
   And every Emir slept in arms;
Crusaders from the ferine west,
   Imbued with mad religious hate;
Were rushing in fanatic zest,
   The Muslim to annihilate.
For Baldwin's brow the diadem
   Of Palestinian empire bound,
The Kingdom of Jerusalem,
   And hallowed Bethlehem's holy ground.
Their legions reached Diyar-bekir,
   And surged around Damascus wall,
And Syrian blood besprent the spear
   In fair Edessa's palace hall;
And rapine followed in their path,
   The pestilence that famine bears,
Haran and Sidon felt their wrath,
   And Tyre and Tripolis were theirs;
No lance to stay the fearful scourge,
   Where Kedron's fairy waters flashed,
Nor champion's voice the Muslims urge
   Where the Orontes droning dashed;
In vain the people sought relief
   From fierce oppression's blighting breath;
And overcome by fear and grief,
   Even the doughtiest prayed for death;
But all was changed when Zengi first
   In battle couched Islamic spear,
And over the Orontes burst
   On his victorious career.
His eye with battle fire aglare,
   His swarthy cheek with triumph flushed;
That blade, Damascus made, was bare,
   And with the blood of foemen blushed.
I saw him on Tiberias plain,
   In youthful ardour lead the van,
When blood distilled like winter rain,

And Mandud led the Mussulman.
'Twas there he played a knightly part,
  And won his spurs on tented field,
And earned the love of every heart
  That homage will to valour yield.
'Mid western knight and Frankish peer,
  And Syria's martial Emir keen,
No more renowned cavalier
  Than gallant, young, Imad-ed-din.
I saw his mettled coursers prance,
  His banners with the Khalif lined,
When Dubeys and his Arab lance,
  On billows swept, incarnadined;
With daring heart Antar, the brave,
  Against him sped in proud array,
To break in pieces, wave on wave,
  The finest swords of Araby.
I seem to see him once again
  Breasting the billows of that sea,
Beneath him dead and dying men;
  The Arab's choicest chivalry;
Before the Sultan's eye that hour,
  Of gentle deed and courtly grace,
The foremost on the run for power,
  Leading the veterans in the race.
It was not there he made his name,
  But by the Jordan's rippling wave;
It was not there undying fame
  Her wreath of greenest laurel gave;
It was not there he was revered,
  But by Orontes turbid tide;
It was not there his name was feared,
  But on the Jordan's western side;
He was the first the torch to light,
  And bid the European pause;
The first to meet the Christian might
  As champion of the Muslim cause.

I think I see the chieftain now,
   By dark Atharib's lofty keep,
The thunders lowering on his brow,
   His eyes where lurid lightnings sleep.
I saw the warlike passion rise
   Upon his brow as morning light!
I saw the fury in his eyes,
   As lightning's thro' the darkest night!
The turbans glittered on the plain,
   Amid the hills the battle flags;
The eagles swooping in our train
   Forsook their eyries on the crags.
We challenged and the foe replied,
   And long withstood us man to man,
For they were warriors picked and tried,
   Of Normandy and Frankistan.
We met defiance with our mines,
   And mangonels the turrets swept,
Closer and closer drew our lines,
   Day after day we nearer crept.
Unto their aid with all his might
   Jerusalem's Christian sovereign came,
He knew those sparks of transient light
   Were heralds of devouring flame;
They came to meet us; 'twas the choice
   Of Prince and baron, banneret;
And we, aroused by Zengi's voice,
   For the assault impatient fret.
The cry, 'Give them a taste of Hell,'
   Was answered from the frowning rock;
And then against the infidel
   Our coursers bounded to the shock;
Into that sea of steel we rode,
   As rivers pouring forth in flood
Our blades a brighter crimson showed
   Than ever sprung from slavish blood;
Onward, as speedy as the wind,

    Charge after charge the Emir led;
They rank before us, and behind
    Ruin a tragic glory spread;
The falchions leapt in tongues of flame
    Where'er our Arab coursers trod,
The bodies of our foes became
    The scabbards of the swords of God!
But few escaped the martyr's crown
    Amid the Frank and Norman peers;
The solemn, silent stars looked down
    On red Atharib's rayless spears.
The Crescent of the Seljukees
    Was floating over every height,
The song of victory on the breeze,
    The clarion of the Islamite.
You yet may know the battlefield,
    For bones are crumbling there to dust,
And riven helm and battered shield,
    Are lying there defaced with rust.
Edessa, lad, his glory made;
    He toyed with Amid, to beguile
The spears of Jocelin; so delayed
    His march at Amid's gates awhile.
Deceived, they went, an erring band,
    And scarce defended left the town,
And we departed by command
    To haul Edessa's crosses down;
As reapers in the field of death,
    As brother Muslims side by side,
To guard the honour of the Faith,
    To bear the brunt, and turn the tide.
Onward to reap the swathes we went,
    Onward to pass the foemen's flank,
Unloosened rein and body bent,
    Bridle by bridle, rank on rank;
Line after line the horsemen go,
    And head by head the chargers run,

With spears and turbans row on row,
   It was a wondrous sight, my son.
The Sun of Islam rose again,
   And on our banners flashed success;
We met the Franks in their domain,
   And paid them for their wickedness;
We stormed Edessa town at last,
   And vengeance whetted every blade.
For every insult of the past,
   A shambles of the place we made;
We would have razed it to the ground,
   Its turrets with the desert laid,
Destroyed its ramparts; but the sound
   Of Zengi's voice the slaughter stayed.
Our Emir's valour thro' the lands
   Was bruited by the Muslim's lips,
And unto distant western strands
   Was carried by the Christian ships.
And yet they slew him, slew the man
   Who from oppression gave relief;
No more his eye the battle scan;
   They slew him! Slew our peerless chief!
No more in front his turban shine;
   The' assassin's dagger pierced his breast,
No more his lance will lead the line,
   Nor sabre scourge the seething west.

Originally published in *The Islamic World*, 1901

The Spirit of God

On the perfume of flowerlets in the dell,
On the white sea-foam on the ocean swell,
On the shivering lances of silvery light,
On the shimmering sunbeam's arrowy flight,
   The Spirit of God is nigh.

Through the ebony night's amorphous veil,
Through the feathery clouds, the starlight pale,
Flutters to earth; and the glimmering rays
Of the gibbous moon, singing His praise,
   The Spirit of God in the sky.

On the silent lake, on the limpid stream,
In the quiet sleep, in the feverish dream,
On the howling storm's tempestuous breast,
On the balmy air, dreaming, at rest,
   The Spirit of God rides high.

Where droning bees their nectar sip,
Where poppies hang o'er the river's lip,
Where the red, red cheek of the roses blush,
Where the flaming cups of tulips flush,
   The Spirit of God doth lie.

   Originally published in *The Crescent*, July 9, 1902

Zola[17]

Mighty the nineteenth century,
   And mighty its giant race,
But slowly the Titans are passing
   Off earth's sepulchral face.

Zola has followed the masters,
   Gone with that century's men
(Ingersoll, Huxley and Darwin),
   Voiceless and still is his pen.

The drifting drift of the tide,
   The scudding scud of the sea,

---

[17] Poem was written to memorialize eminent French writer Émile Zola (1840-1902).

The billowy billows of life,
   The dirging dirge we dree.

The drift of the tide has ceased,
   The wreck on the shore is cast,
Star-streaming banners of night
   Are over him gliding at last.

Returns no more the flower
   That hath once shed its bloom;
There is no returning
   Through the gateway of the tomb.

   Originally published in *The Crescent*, October 15, 1902

The Dirge We Dirging Dree

   A birth,
   A momentary flash,
   A blaze of sunshine,
   A cloud of melancholy,
   A parting gleam—
   Then death.

Like to drift of the drifting tide,
   To scud of the scudding sea,
To billows on the billowy wide,
   Is the dirge we dirging dree.

Like to lash of the lashing hail,
   The breath of the breathing sea,
To fiery dust when on dusty trail,
   Streams of streaming star-shot flee.

Like to drone of the droning blast,
   The moan of the moaning bay,
To the shadow of shadows cast

By beam of the beaming day.

Like to white of the whitest light,
   Deep scent of scented flowers,
To the black of the blackest night,
   Black musk of musky bowers.

Like to 'plash of the 'plashing stream,
   Red-gold on a golden hair,
To the fever of feverish dream,
   To balm in the balmy air.

To the break of the breaking wave,
   To wave of the waving tree,
To the still of the stilly grave,
   Is the dirge we dirging dree.

Kilwinning, Scotland

Originally published in *The Crescent*, October 22, 1902

The Song of the Despondent Lover

O, why hast thou left me, love?
   Why art thou gone away?
Now I must wander alone, love,
   Far over moorland and brae.

Do you remember the night
When in the moon's pale light,
   By the Garnock's gurgling stream,
Our souls were blended together,
Joined as if for ever
   By love's happiest dream?

For love, sweet love, was dawning,
   And O! but thy heart was gay,

But now the dreamer you're scorning—
   Love's passion is fading away.

Beneath spheres celestial turning
Of starry lanes, when burning
   In night's abyssmal bowl
Love's vials do thicken and gather,
Filled with passion-drops, bitter as Marah,
   Blighting and shriveling my soul.

Beyond the paths of Reason
   Love's heights I climbed to thee,
But now the paths of Reason
   No more I'll ever see

Athwart that soul a pall is hurled,
Spawn-vomited from a nether world
   An infernal incubus up-steaming;
Can nought on earth that pain assuage?
Which Orcan fires within me rage,
   The dreamer has finished his dreaming.

Originally published in *The Crescent*, November 5, 1902

Ez Zegri[18]

See, 'tis the gleaming of armour!
   Behold the glitter of spears!
Muslim cohorts advancing,
   Islam's noblest peers.

Graceful the curving of war-steed,
   Graceful the tilting of lance,

---

[18] A tribute to the Zegri clan, a Moorish family of nobles in the fifteenth-century kingdom of Granada. Their defeat in 1492 is regarded as the end of Muslim rule in Spain.

Proudly the banners are streaming,
  And proudly the horsemen prance.

Ever the foremost in conflict,
  Foemen before them shall reel,
Ruby drops drip from their lances,
  Crimson the glare of their steel.

Death's in the cup that they offer,
  And deep shall each foeman drain,
When that the music of battle
  Pours forth its martial refrain.

Thy deeds, O Granada, the peerless!
  Round Islam's heart shall entwine,
Engraved on her banners of learning,
  Bright stars that eternal shine.

Dark is the eye of the chieftain,
  And dark 'gainst his turban's fold
Flashes his lady-love's favour,
  Jet black on the glittering gold.

Flower of Mussulman knighthood,
  Gallant in charge or in chase,
Prince of the Beni Zegri,
  The pride of Granada's race.

Onward, then, the Campeador's
  'Gainst Espana's dons do go,
Caballeros, Granadinos,
  Nurtured 'neath Nevada's snow.

  Originally published in *The Crescent*, November 19, 1902

An Inspiration

Dark is the life of a single man
  And lonely his lot when boarding.
No one to brighten his rayless path,
  No one his cash to be hoarding.

While doleful hours are passing,
  And weeks they onward roll,
A cloud black as Orcus is crossing
  Athwart the disk of his soul.

He seeks, but he finds her not,
  A *true* woman of his admiration.
And in search of his *ideal* soars
  To the stars for an inspiration.

For he longs for a passionate love,
  Longs for a love that is *living*,
A love that is stronger than death,
  Throbbing with passion, life giving.

He dreams of a heart that is true,
  And yearns for a love that's abiding,
For the glamour of a roguish eye,
  Or of pouting lips when chiding.

Ye gifted and poetic maidens,
  He shall accept one *al hazar*,
So if you want to be wedded,
  Apply ye to…

Originally published in *The Crescent*, November 26, 1902

With Apologies to Sheikh Abdullah Quilliam Effendi, Sheikh-ul-Islam[19]

"He had been dreaming, and was chilled to the
bone. Wretchedness, mental and bodily, took hold of
him. Well, often enough such is the fate of those
who dream; those who turn from their needful, daily
tasks to shape an angel out of this world's clay, trusting
to some unknown god to give it life and spirit"—
(Henry Rider Haggard in "Stella Fregelius," in *T.P.'s Weekly*, No.2)

"Get wed, get wed," the poet says,
   In strong sentiment ecstatic,
You will have joyful, joyful days
   (In language most emphatic).

As streams of bliss around you pour,
   Drowning your bitterest sorrow,
Bright will be the hours galore
   If you get wed to-morrow.

Say, O say, where the *houris* dwell
   Deserving such great admiration;
Are they celestial beings, tell,
   Or some freaks of imagination?

Are they the inane things in dress
   That parade for show to church?
Do they exist in the awful press,
   Where slithering wrecks on pavement lurch?

In *furor poeticus* say where they dwell,
   Language throbbing with passionate ringing,
For us no Circe entrancing spell,

---

[19] Poem was in response to Sheikh Abdullah Quilliam's poem "Some Good Advice to Single Men" (Page 147)

We want no sirens singing.

Bring them to light, O Sheikh-ul-Islam,
   To light with thy redolent pen
Engraved on the folds of thy oriflamme,
   And we shall find them men.

Originally published in *The Crescent*, December 3, 1902

A Ballad of Chivalry

Beneath Andalu's sky,
   In pale stars' feeble light,
A host of banners fly
   O'er men in armour bright.
   In darkness of the night
They gather on the plain,
   De Leon and his might,
The chivalry of Spain.

In splendid panoply
   Those warriors bedight,
Against the Moor they hie,
   For battle's their delight.
   Hidalgo, serf and knight,
The Cross for to maintain,
   "For Jesus and the Right,"
The chivalry of Spain.

'Mid Ronda mountains high,
   That makes each cheek turn white,
Hark to that fearful cry
   Ringing from height to height:
   "Ez Zagel! To the fight!"
They seek escape in vain,
   They fall both left and right,
The chivalry of Spain.

Envoi—
O! 'twas a wondrous sight
   To see that gorgeous train
In terror-stricken flight,
   The chivalry of Spain.

Belfast, April 4, 1903

Originally published in *The Crescent*, April 29, 1903

On the Dee

We bore along the regal stream
   At falling of the day,
Our oarsmen they were Cameron
   And Billal Quilliam Bey,
Professor Preston seized the helm,
   To steer us on our way,
And Trainor thought "the water wet"
   As we flew on 'mid spray

Upon our left the grand old town
   Of Chester rose on high,
Whose walls had oft in olden time
   Re-echoed battle-cry
When warlike princes of the Welsh,
   With valour's blazing eye,
Their warriors 'gainst the Norman led
   To conquer or to die

How glorious the evening was,
   How sweet to be afloat,
With beauty all around you and
   With *beauty* in your boat
Our oarsmen pulled the faster 'long,
   With quick and rhythmic rote,
Adown the Royal River Dee,

That once was Chester's moot.

Originally published in *The Crescent*, July 29, 1903

Love-Dreams

The smiling moon in highest heaven did ride
'Mid circling fields of star-dust spreading wide;
My love and I, beneath an olden tower,
In dreams of love outpaced each racing hour.

With Luna o'er us cast a silver veil
Begemm'd with starry emblems, golden pale;
And love it filled each ivy-festoon'd bower—
The very air was charged with magic power.

We sat in silence 'neath the crumbling wall,
And gazed with awe upon its arches tall,
Thro' which, in warlike might, the Baron bold
Rode forth, girdled with steel and spurr'd with gold.

And strong moss-troopers 'long the drawbridge sprung,
Till helmet, lance, cuirass and buckle rung;
While ladies, from deep windows ivy-laced,
Waved scarfs to noble knights in mail encased.

I turned and looked into my lady's eyes,
And they were deep as blue of Paradise,
And soft and gentle as Narcissus flower,
Distilling love with tender fresh'ning shower.

I touched her lips, and pressed her golden hair,
I kissed a cheek than Sharon's Rose more fair,
A brow, e'en than the lotus fairer blows,
A bosom whiter than Idalian snows.

Come, then, my love, and as the hours go by
We'll dream of love, true love, that ne'er can die;
Once more our holy pledge we will renew,
One single thought, one soul, atween us two.

Fair Luna o'er us spreads her web of lawn;
Within its folds we'll lie till morning dawn;
Entangled in the flowing robe of Night,
The fleeting hours shall o'er us wing their flight.

Originally published in *The Crescent*, August 12, 1903

Jemal-ud-deen Bokhari Jeffery[20]

A Memorial Ode

His bark's at rest
Beyond the crest
Of the horizon's bars,
In gentle breeze
On sunless seas,
'Mid peeping forth of stars.

A noble life
Has ceased its strife,
A soul has winged its flight
To Paradise
Amid the wise,
O'er harbour bar of night.

---

[20] Jemal-ud-deen Bokhari Jeffery (1830-1903) had been a friend of Sheikh Abdullah Quilliam since 1873. He became an early supporter of the Liverpool Muslims and then a convert in 1889. He was an integral member of the Liverpool Moslem Institute, serving at various times as librarian, secretary, and vice-president, as well as often lecturing. Most importantly, he was put in charge of the Institute's affairs when the Sheikh was away.

    Pale lilies spread
    Above his head
Bedew his grave with tears.
    The life of man
    Is but a span
Within the circling years.

    An angel breath,
    The dew of death,
With God to be above;
    The home of peace,
    Where struggles cease,
In halls of 'lasting love.

    The storm that raves
    Shall calm its waves,
And tides shall ebb their flood;
    New suns shall rise,
    And cross our skies,
And set again in blood.

Originally published in *The Crescent*, October 7, 1903

In the Gloom

Dark was the track of the night o'er the wild wood,
    Loud was the howl of the wind thro' the trees,
Rolled were the clouds on the breast of the blue vault,
    Cold was the breath of the frost-laden breeze.

Deep in the heart of the mists high in cloudland,
    Locked in their bosom the black thunder lay,
High o'er the tops of the tall pines in woodland
    Wild the red tongues of the forked lightings play.

Drear is the path thro' those depths deep and lonesome,
    Fast on the branches the rain-drops they lash,

Strong thro' the centre of night's seething entrails
   Bolts of the thunder they leap, roar and crash.

Black on my soul lay the foul breath of midnight,
   Black as the trees that in grim phantoms start,
Poured forth in gloom from deep wells full of sorrow
   Fumes from the depths of a sad, stricken heart.

Flame thro' the rift in yon vortex so awful,
   Fly on the track of the whirlwind's pale breath,
Roam, O, ye fiends, in the bowels of nightland,
   Lay low your plumes in the ghoul-haunts of death.

Originally published in *The Crescent*, October 14, 1903

Almansur (1)[21]

From Cordova's smiling fountains,
   From Elvira's winter snows,
Sea-beat coast and inland mountains,
   Pressing northward 'gainst the foe
   Andalusia's banners go.

Onward, on to victory passing,
   O'er the crest of tufted hill,
Scimetars and lances flashing,
   Soon of death to drink their fill,
   Pouring forth in ruddy rill.

Through Cantabria's mountains far
   Pierced Almansûr's Moorish lance
Through Leon, Castile and Navarre
   Moordom's noblest emirs prance,

---

[21] Al-Mansur Bi'llah (938-1002) (known as Almanzor in Spanish accounts) was the de facto ruler of Andalusia from 978-1002. He led dozens of expeditions against the Spanish Christians.

Eastern banners gaily dance.

Sons of Islām, knight, commander,
   Line on line they outward span,
With the lance of great Almansûr
   Glittering in the Muslim van,
   Defender of the law, Kurān.

Scourge of thy foeman, soldier of Hishām,
   Victorious wert thou in every campaign,
Greatest sword that ever Islām
   Launched o'er ringing fields of Spain,
   Ever drenched her bleeding plain.

In earth's embrace now calmly sleeping,
   O'er war's red ranks thy banners wave
No more, nor rolling Tekbir sweeping,
   Low lies the chief, the dauntless brave;
   Plant tall cypress o'er his grave.

Originally published in *The Crescent*, May 6, 1903

Verses

Half-hidden I lay in a hollow,
   'Mid the glare of the spears of the hay;
Above me twittered the swallow,
   As it glided and skimmed on its way;
Afar with a waft of its wing
   It threaded the air in its flight,
And the aerial sea, like a king,
   It breasted, a speck in the light.

High over me towered a ruin,
   In the tragical glory of years,
With dungeons that grass never grew in,
   But enriched with the splendour of tears;

On the top of the wall was a flower
   That was blooming alone 'mid the leaves,
Still wet with the breath of a shower;
   And the swallows they built in the eaves.

Once again when the Autumn in glory
   Spread its gold on the brow of the year;
To that desolate tower so hoary
   I came with foreboding and fear;
And the scythe of the reaper had shone,
   And the gleaner had gathered the sheaves;
And the flower and its beauty were gone;
   And the swallow deserted the caves.

Kilwinning, Scotland

   Originally published in *The Crescent*, March 30, 1904

The Poet's Dream

By a ruined tower olden,
   Lay the poet idly dreaming;
'Neath him fields with gowans golden,
   O'er him skies were gently streaming.

Sparkling streamlets, foaming whitely,
   O'er the cascade downward flowing,
On their lips red poppies brightly
   In the sunshine beauteous glowing.

Sweetly summer it was breathing,
   Blooming, balmy crimson roses;
Fairy fingers deftly weaving.
   Spreading carpets, bunching posies.

Laverocks in the sky were winging
   Dark against its silver brightness,

And to earth were clearly singing
   Lyrics of a tender lightness.

Here and there a covey started
   From a rugged knoll of heather,
Here and there a blackbird darted
   Glitt'ring suns on every feather.

Originally published in *The Crescent*, April 13, 1904

A Dream

What an anguishing trial is life,
   With its doubts and its fears and its woes,
When misery is ever so rife,
   And it breathes in the wind as it blows;
For the night's on the disk of my soul,
   And my heart's in the sorrowful past,
And the passions they surge and they roll,
   And emotions o'ercome me at last.

I sat by the wayside alone,
   And I dreamt of the things that had been,
I thought on the days that had flown,
   Of the days and the nights I had seen;
Of the love I had given and lost,
   Of the rage on a handsome face,
The flush of a cheek, where tossed
   The blood of the Teuton race.

The dew it was damp on the thorn,
   And the breath of the evening was chill;
And I sat, all alone and forlorn,
   On the stone at the foot of the hill;
And a vision I saw in repose,
   A view of a face I had known;
Of a cheek with the glow of the rose,

And hair that was carelessly thrown;

Of a girlish face that was fair,
  And a neck that was pure and white;
Of a head with its golden hair,
  Of an eye that was tender and bright,
Of breasts that were whiter than snow,
  And of lips that were tempting and red,
Of a love that in beauty did grow,
  Of a love 'twas forsaken and fled;

Of a love that was honest and true,
  Of a heart that is now grown cold,
Of evenings of anguish and rue,
  And of mornings of roses and gold;
Of the day, with its raptures and fears;
  Of night, with its whispers of love;
Of shadows, of sighs and of tears,
  'S if bolts had been shot from above.

When the gardens were bright with the flowers,
  And the roses of love were in bloom,
And Cheiranthus, distilling its showers,
  Shone 'mid glory and splendour and gloom;
But it waned with the death of the morn,
  Like a spectral lamp in a room,
And the flame of its virtue was shorn,
  Till it glowed as of mist o'er a tomb.

Originally published in *The Crescent*, October 5, 1904

Muslim Battle-Song

Sons of the East, children of Araby,
Flashing your spears, tossing your banners gay;
On to the war Modhar and Yemen go,
Swords in the air, laying the foemen low,

Swift as a bird, dense as the drifting sand,
Onward they fly, following band on band.

Men of the North, Cays and Kurayish there,
Foremost in fight, bred in the desert air;
War-cubs at play, cheeks with the battle flush,
Breasting the plain, on to their prey they rush;
Trample and slay, joyful in braving death,
Knowing no fear, brave to their latest breath.

Far in the fight, leading the raging van,
Banners of green, outward their sweeping span;
Screaming on high over the conflict dread
Vultures aloft, circling far overhead;
Steel that was clear shone in the morning bright,
Swords that were red pale in the evening light.

Originally published in *The Crescent*, January 11, 1905

H.I.M. Abdul-Hamid Ghazi Khan, Sultan of Turkey, Emir-el-Mumooneen[22]

Great son of Osman's glorious line,
Long may thy Star and Crescent shine;
Long may thy flag the tempest ride,
Tho' winds of war be circling wide;
May victory for ever grace
The sword of Osman's royal race.
The Phoenix loves the spicy bower,
But thou, O Chief, the battle stour;
Not birks where fragrant odours dwell;
But bowers of steel, 'mid battle yell;
The tramp of men, the neighing steed,
The tekbir roll, the knightly deed.

---

[22] Abdul Hamid II (1842-1918) was the Ottoman Sultan contemporary with the activities of the Liverpool Muslims. He ruled from 1876-1909.

Of great Mahommed's stem a shoot,
A branch of Islam's fertile root;
A shoot of power, a branch of might,
The Conqueror's fires in thee relight;
The fire that burned when Sulieman
The trembling west with troops o'erran;
With flaunting banners, sturdy spears,
Nor Christendom produced their peers.
Those dauntless men of generous wrath,
As rivers sweep they swept a path;
E'en as the rose is first of flowers,
So they were first of warlike powers;
E'en as the lily's cup is white,
Their shields with honour, clear and bright;
E'en as the tulip's flame is red
They blood of foemen duteous shed.
No age but their's produced such lords,
No other age bore nobler swords;
In ardent youth's unclouded light,
The virgin dawn compared to night;
Their strength by Khalid's soul empowered,
Their steel in combat wild deflowered.
As strong as eagles winged in flight,
Their banners soared aloft in fight;
They trod the path by Allah given
As wandering moons tread over heaven;
A path illumed by valour's ray,
As circling suns illume the day.
The night's dark veil festoon'd with stars,
Their veil a host of scimitars;
A blaze of steel, the lightning's breath,
The glare of day, oblivion, death;
Engraven deep on history's page,
Their deeds, the hope of every age.
The glories of Iconium field
Effulgent made thy father's shield;
And laurels Nicopolis gave

To Ilderim the true and brave;
And Plevna loud with pealing praise
Like thunder of imperial days,
When Turkish banners were unfurled
In warlike pride before the world;
When thronging squadrons lightly mailed,
By heroes led, o'er foes prevailed;
When the Osmanli martial ire
Enkindled with consuming fire
A hundred thousand throbbing breasts,
A thousand fields of tossing crests.

Brave son of Islam, tho' in fight
Thy banners shine, unclouded, bright;
May peace with honour be thy part,
The aim of every noble heart.
Remember how the Prophet wrought,
And follow well the words he taught;
Strong for the right, but slow to wrath,
Tread Abu Bekr's earnest path.
Triumphant splendour then will grace
The generous deed of generous race;
And honours round thy throne entwine,
Enhance the glories of thy line.
An empire's treasures in thy hand,
Be thou their guide and guarding brand;
Be thine the Khalif's faithful part,
And thine the true parental heart;
To rule the nation, guard the laws,
Thy people's good their sovereign's cause,
In joy and woe, in peace and war,
Be thou their light and pilot star;
The hope of all the good and true,
The light Abdallah's offspring knew;
The light that flashed on scroll of gold,
When over Hira thunder rolled;
The scroll that bore the nomes of light

In vision on Al-Kadar night;
The night of power when joy is born
And all is peace till rosy morn.
Hail! Osman's scion, strong of arm,
To shield thy people from all harm;
The bird of time is winging fast,
Our actions live when we have past;
'Tis thine to act the kingly part,
The warm unfettered royal heart;
Let love unite with sovereign grace,
Thy name shall gain immortal place;
The towers wherein thy fathers sleep
Thy sons maintain and ever keep;
Salaam, Emir, faithful stand,
Be truth and right thy high command.
—I remain, O Emir-el-Mumooneen, thy humble and obedient servant.

Originally published in *The Crescent*, April 19, 1905

Almansur (2)[23]

O'er the hills of Andalusia
   Rings the Arab battle-cry,
Fast Islamic spearmen gather,
   There Omeya's banners fly;
Great Almansûr leads to battle
   Cordova's effulgent shields;
Victor o'er his Christian foemen
   In a hundred tented fields;
Never did a doughtier leader
   Guard the sacred law Kuran;
O'er the Muslim spears in battle
   Eagle-eyed the conflict scan;
Where the sunshine it was sparkling

---

[23] See note on page 75 for information concerning Almansur.

On the point of steel'd lance;
'Mid their sternest legions pressing
   'Gainst the knights of Spain and France.
Thro' the heart of the Austurias,
   Thro' the mountains of Navarre,
In a hurricane of fury
   Swept the hero's helms afar;
Shrieked the north in sudden anguish
   Where the warrior turned his course,
Desolation, desolation,
   Trodden by the Moorish horse.
Fifty-two campaigns the chieftain
   'Gainst his northern foemen led;
And his spearmen rode to conquest,
   Trampling every pathway red.
In the dust Navarre is lying,
   Castile bleeds at every pore;
For Abdallah's mighty scion
   Islam's banner proudly bore.
With the swordsmen of Elvira,
   Cordova's renowned lance;
Where Toledo's troops are dashing,
   Saragossa's Emirs prance.
O'er the wreck of wild Commarcas
   Line on line the Muslims sped;
Not a foe dare stand for battle,
   Not a Christian raise his head;
For the eastern turbans glittered,
   And the clarion tekbir ran;
When the lance of great Almansûr
   Led the Moorish battle-van.

Originally published in *The Crescent*, June 21, 1905

To His Excellency W.H. Abdullah Quilliam Bey Effendi

A Knight
"*Sans pour et sans reproche*"
This Poem Is Lovingly Inscribed

No chevalier more courteous and refined
For Islam's cause e'er stood in tourney ring;
The laurel wreath around his turban twined,
His pen is nobler than the sword of king;
And Europe owns no gentlier, doughtier knight,
No better drew for Bourbon, Stuart or Guelf,
A Bayard he of kind and generous might;
Abdullah is nobility itself.
Not his, triumphal arch that some desire,
Nor his, the warrior's wondrous pageantry;
But his, the hand to wield the pen of fire,
And his, the poet's crown of greenest bay.
Osmanieh, no nobler ever wore,
Medjidieh, more glorious never bore.

Originally published in *The Crescent*, August 9, 1905

The Last Great Moor[24]

Ten thousand tents along the valley spread,
A thousand Caballeros battle-bred;
The sun shone bright on spear and shield and helm,
The noblest swords in fair España's realm;
Ferdinand and his Queen with all their might,
Navarre's proud lord and Castile's reckless knight.
They came from north and south, and east and west,
Of Christendom, the doughtiest and the best,

---

[24] An account of Musa ibn Abu l'Gazan, the lone Muslim to refuse to capitulate to the Spanish forces of King Ferdinand and Queen Isabella after the protracted siege of Granada. His true fate is unknown, but this poem depicts the legend of his last stand.

For their religion's sake the lance to wield
Against the Moor on Andalusian field;
Against Granada town, with arms to strive
The Moorish king of land and crown deprive.
Without the walls in pomp of war unrolled,
Of silken tent, steel, mail, and crests of gold;
And, with Ferdinand, Isabella came,
And all her Court, Castillian maid and dame.
The veteran of a hundred fights was there,
The youth still ill at ease when swords are bare
The first, to stir anew a failing flame,
The second, win his spurs and make a name.
Before their might the Muslim cities fell,
Whose ruins yet of former splendour tell.
Beneath the bitter sky she stood forlorn
Granada, of her trapping shorn;
The beauties of the morning once were hers,
The knightliest knights who ere wore golden spurs.
An Eastern gem in Western setting placed,
Her chevaliers the Courts of Europe graced;
From lance and helmet bar the trophies hung,
And troubadours of wondrous prowess sung;
First in the tourney ring with sword and spear,
No woman's hand might stay their proud career.
Abdallah, in Alhambra palace great,
Surrounded by his nobles, sat in State;
Each downcast look told news with danger fraught,
Yusuf, Ferdinand's proclamation brought.
He heard the terms the Christians would accept,
Dishonoured, many a famous Emir wept.
Amid that throng one eye looked on in ire,
One chieftain's eye alone flashed fire;
The flower of all Granada's youthful might,
Muza Ben Abil Gazan, first in fight.
He rose, and every eye the light forsook,
They feared the general's scornful look.
A death-like stillness fell on one and all,

An instant's pause in Great Alhambra hall.
Then, even as the solemn thunder moans
Along the sky, came deep his martial tones;
A heart of temper tried by years of strife,
To whom a stainless name was more than life.
"These downcast eyes are not for Granadine,
A craven he who dreads a foe unseen.
Come leave to child and maid those useless tears,
Have we not arms, shields, scimitars and spears?
For home and hearth have we not hearts to feel?
And bosoms to withstand the foeman's steel?
Let war, devouring as the simoom's fire,
Now swallow ranks of men, the son and sire.
Arise, ye Muslim lords, 'tis not too late
To stem the tide, set free again the state;
And let the generations yet to be
Tell how we died to set our country free.
Death comes to all, nor tells the hour or year;
Azrael's wings o'er shadow each one here,
What fear ye then? Unto the noble heart
One refuge still remains, the hero's part,
Who for his freedom, children and wife,
And for his native land, gives up his life.
If Castile's king thinks we the distaff wield,
Then let him know we bear the lance and shield;
With every breast for freedom beating warm,
In every heart the passion of the storm.
Up! Muslims, up! arm, arm, each stalwart youth,
Two hundred thousand swords to strike for truth;
And prove our father's blood is running yet
Thro' every vein, we sons of Arab grit;
The offspring of a sturdy race of old
Who cast on high their pennons flaunting gold.
We shall not starve while 'fore us lies a land
With milk and honey ready to our hand.
Then send us forth against th' apostate brood,
Our horse are swift and they will find us food;

Or we beneath beloved Granada's wall
A soldier's death shall seek, for Islam fall.
Behold our women, see each pleading maid,
Their eyes demand a husband, father's aid.
And shall they plead in vain? For shame ye men,
Gird on your armour, seize your swords again;
Dishonoured will you see them? captives led,
A foeman's thrall for alien board and bed;
Your mosques disgraced by unbelieving bands,
Your shrines profaned by sacrilegious hands;
Your faith forbidden; for each loyal heart
The torture chamber; fire and rack your part,
Wake sons of Islam, great Granada's lords;
Wake sons of Islam, grasp again your swords."
The chieftain paused, all motionless as death,
So still they sat you scarcely heard a breath;
Contempt dwelt for an instant on his face,
He saw the degradation of his race.
The anger deepened on his brow's high mound,
His flashing eye looked scorn on all around;
Erect the warrior drew his manly form,
While on his brow still darker lower'd the storm;
His kindling fury trembled in each nerve,
To think his race from battle shock should swerve;
Sons of illustrious birth, in knightly wrath
Their fathers swept whole legions from their path;
Too feeble now to play a fearless part,
Long years of ease had weakened every heart.
Again his clarion tones rang clear and strong,
Thro' pillared vistas echoed loud and long.
"Men of illustrious blood, Granada's peers,
Nasirine princes, Zegris noblest spears;
Abencerrages, chieftains good and true,
No knightlier swords did foeman's blood imbrue;
More glorious deeds on history's pages trace.
Untarnished keep the 'scutcheon of thy race;
Were it not better should our city fall

That we lie buried 'neath her ruined wall,
Than live to brook dishonour and disfame
To hear our sons in scorn pronounce our name.
Ye Muslims will ye live to fawn nor fear?
For I shall never craven murmur hear;
To find a grave beneath Alhambra towers
Were sweeter than a couch within her bowers,
To perish fighting in the battle van
The worthy son of worthy Mussulman.
Befitting son of sires, who loved in strife,
When old, to yield to ruthless brand their life;
Those fearless lions made this land their own,
And clad with power the glories of the throne;
A land elate with joy and southern air,
And queen of queens and fairest of the fair;
They built these towers, proud and magnificent,
And chivalry its golden splendour lent;
The groves whose vernal verdure scents the gale,
They planted on each plain and happy vale,
And shall they pass to Christians? Can you bear?
For I will not: by Allah's might I swear,"
He ceased; the echoes fell from sigh to sigh.
The nobles moved not; all afraid to die,
Contemptuous thro' their ranks with haughty grace
Impatient strode the warrior from the place,
On thro' the lion court he passed, nor deigned
To throw a glance; at last he reached his home,
And bade them bring his horse equipped for fight;
His strongest lance and falcion, keen and bright;
His suite of choicest mail, Damascus made.
What oft in fight had turned the stoutest blade;
While yet the sombre council sat in state,
The bravest Moor dashed thro' Elvira gate.
The sun was setting 'yond Nevada's hills.
The wind breathed soft to all the idling rills;
A shady vale amid the mountains lay,
Where rapid Xenil flashed along its way;

With rugged rock and mighty boulder strewn,
While underneath the snowy spray was blown;
And eddying current over pools unsounded,
Where swirling, hissing water plunged and bounded,
Above a track, well worn on lone hillside,
Adown the path a half score warriors ride,
As trusty knights as ever couched a lance
'Neath the flag of Spain, or Oriflamme of France.
No danger signals lit the western sky,
No portents blazed, nor storm-cloud hovered nigh;
No trailing mist, the sun was low and bright,
The jeweled spray sparkled with rainbow light;
The softest laughter rippled on the breeze,
And died in music 'mid the orange trees;
The ear by lullaby of songsters charmed,
The heart by every tender passion warmed.
But hark! A horse's hoofs now spurn the rocks in wrath,
The haughty sons have lined to bar the path;
A single horseman comes, from head to heel
Completely sheathed in coat of finest steel.
"Hold up, sir knight," the foremost Christians cry,
The hills alone return a faint reply;
"Hold up, sir knight, Castillian's here, we say."
Hark, "Allahu Ackbar," the trumpets bray.
The reins fall loose upon the charger's back,
The steel-shod hoofs strike fire along the track,
The nostrils swell almost to bursting point,
The cord-like muscles taut at every joint;
The good horse bounds with speed that faster grows,
Like long pent storm the Moor is on his foes;
Like star from height of outer space he flies,
And low as dust a proud hidalgo lies;
Wheeling his barb, bare is his scimitar,
Lance rings on shield, swords class on visor bar;
They press around him, nine good men to one,
The blades repeat the glory of the sun.
"Surrender noble Moor," they cry, in vain,

He answers not, but blows the faster rain;
Wounded or dead are half his foemen laid,
With tireless sweep his good Toledo blade,
Unerring find at every turn a breast,
Parries a thrust, or cleaves adventurous crest;
His shield is shattered by the shower of blows,
Great dints upon his armour gory shows;
His wounded charger sinks and yields its life,
He gains his feet, renews again the strife.
Still three to one the strokes with vigor rain,
Before the storm his blade is snapped in twain;
He sinks upon his knees before the gale,
His life-blood pouring thro' his broken mail.
One effort more, from blood he clears his sight,
Springs to his feet, unsheathes his dagger bright;
One bound, a glittering streak, descends the knife,
Another foeman is bereft of life;
His war-cry woke the hills and quailed the foe,
He turned and sprang into the stream below;
The waters close, the white spray wings its flight,
Over Ben Abil Gazan, peerless knight,
"Allahu Ackbar—God alone is great,"
He cried, and lover-like embraced his fate;
His honour, like the sun, for ever sure,
He died as Muslim should, the last great Moor.

Originally published in *The Crescent*, August 9, 1905

I Sat by the Wayside Alone

What a rending of hearts is a life,
   With its crosses and losses and woes;
In the dark, in the light they are rife,
   They are borne on the wind as it blows;
For the gloom of the night's on my soul,
   And my heart's in the days that are past,
And the billows of ocean unroll

'Neath the might of the terrible blast.

As I sat by the wayside alone,
  How I dreamt of the things that had been;
How I dwelt on the days that had flown
  And the nights of wild rapture between,
Of the love I had given and lost,
  Of the scorn on a beautiful face,
Of a flush of a maiden whose boast
  Was the blood of a dominant race.

The dewdrops besprinkled the thorn,
  And the breath of the ev'ning was chill,
As I sat all alone and forlorn
  On a stone at the foot of a hill,
Where a vision I saw in repose,
  The surprise of a face I had known,
Of a cheek with the bloom of the rose,
  Sunlit hair that was ruffled and blown.

Ay, to see her was last of my joys,
  Hers a neck of a ravishing hue,
Hers a head with the queenliest poise,
  And an eye that was meltingly blue;
And the form, that to me was divine,
  Was a star that the distance endears;
She, an angel so fragile and fine,
  Is unworn by the tale of the years.

Mine a love that was honest and true,
  Hers a heart that was haughtily cold;
Mine the ev'nings of bitterest rue,
  Hers the mornings when roses unfold;
Mine the day with its tremulous fears,
  To the gloaming my whispers were sigh'd;
Closing clouds rained a passion of tears,
  Nor the tempest its levin denied.

When the garden was pied with the flowers,
   And the roses were heavy in bloom,
And cheiranthus dispensing its showers
   'Mid the chequer of glory and gloom,
My hope waned like the star of the morn,
   Or a flickering lamp in a room,
And the flame of its 'fulgence was shorn,
   And the flare of the day was its tomb.

Kilwinning

Originally published in *The Crescent*, November 8, 1905

Abdallah Ez Zagal at Fez[25]

Leave me children, leave me striplings, mock ye not the aged now,
Once I was as proud as any with a helmet on my brow.
What? Ye tell me I am boasting, that I never drew a blade,
Never for a lady's favour in the tourney foeman laid.
Have ye heard of Rhonda mountains, yonder in the Spanish land?
How the troops of Don Rodrigro fell before the Muslim brand?
I was there that day of triumph, in the thickest of the fray,
When España's best and bravest on the mountains dying lay.
Still ye mock me? See the scars! They are the proofs that I advance,
That in days of youthful ardour I have borne Islamic lance;
Where the Prophet's banner flaunted, and the faithful rallied round,
I have stood 'mid dead and dying on the battle cumbered ground.
Blind! They blinded me, my foemen; Allah grant again my sight,
Eyes and arms as strong as ever, when I led my spears in fight.
'Tis the truth, ye knaves, I tell you; know ye not a Moorish lord?

---

[25] Abu 'Abdullah Muhammad az-Zaghall (Muhammad XIII) was a successful general before briefly becoming the Sultan of Granada (1485-1486). He was replaced by his nephew Abu 'Abdullah Muhammad (Muhammad XII) who promptly capitulated to the Spanish Christians. Az-Zaghall left for North Africa, where he was blamed for the fall of Granada and imprisoned in Fez. There he was tortured and blinded.

Have your fathers never told you how they feared Ez Zagal's sword?
Hearken to the mob of cowards; listen to their mocking cheers;
Dogs who dare not meet my sabre when I led Granada's peers.
Allah, but an instant grant me, I may bear the lance and glaive;
I will prove to them, Abdallah still can head the battle wave.
Dotard am I? I remember in those days of wild delight,
Not a shield in Christian Europe could withstand my lance in fight.
Now begone! Ye worthless rabble! Will ye mock a sightless man?
Scorning thus a helpless warrior who has led the Muslim van.
Heard ye not how proud Hidalgos when we met in friendly hour,
Doffed their helmets to Ez Zagal as a tribute to his power?
Hear I not the tramp of chargers? Can I Merwan's scions trace?
Have the lions of Omeya left the palace of their race?
It is so; they died like heroes; heroes fighting till they fell;
Even yet their memory lingers, of their glory still we tell.
What! Abdallah, are you wandering? Has your fate unhinged your
    mind?
Why! O why, you base protector; did you make Ez Zagal blind?
Oh, my God! I cannot see thee, but I feel thee, trusty blade;
Many a score of Christian foemen on the sward you stricken laid.
What? You jeer again, you scoffers, one who bled in Islam's cause?
Have you never read his teachings or practised the Prophet's laws?
Has the chivalry we taught you, been forgotten in a day?
Is Granada's martial glory lost in ruin and decay?
Had you followed great Ez Zagal we had held Alhambra's tower;
Beaten off the Catholic sovereigns, and restored the Muslim power.
I have known the days, ye caitiffs, when I rode on battlefields,
With a thousand knights behind me and in front a thousand shields;
I have seen the morning sunshine shining on the lines of spears;
I have seen the evening crimson and a rain of women's tears.
Brave Alonzo; wise Gonzalo; ye were cast in knightly mould;
Cienfuetos; Santiago; faithful friends, and foemen bold;
We have met amid the carnage; oft in tourney ring we drew;
Side by side with Cid Alnayer, and Ben Egas staunch and true.
Never more the Bivarambla will resound with Moorish song;
Never more the Beni Zeraj proudly on the causeway throng;
Never more Alhambra palace with the shout of Allah ring;

Never more a Beni Nasir gird his sword and ride a king.
They have gone, the gallant, noble; they have furled their fighting
   flags;
They have left alone, the eagles on the Alpuxarras crags;
Gone to join their mighty fathers, men whom brave Alhamar led;
Buried with Granada's glory, numbered with her dauntless dead.
Why am I not there beside them, lying with the honoured brave?
Royal blood should stream in battle, never creep in veins of slave.
Why did I not perish, Hamet, noble Zegri; on that day;
When you stood on Gibalfaro like a Muslim lord at bay?
Scorned by slaves, the people jeer me, well they know my want of
   sight;
When I rode with thee Ben Egas; then they feared Ez Zagal's might.
O to see again Granada with the Vega stretching far,
And the Darro flashing onward, fairer than the morning star;
Once again in tourney contest bear on high the victor's lance;
Or to awful shock of conflict, bid the Moorish lines advance;
Once again to lead, the chevaliers I led in days of old,
When the cry of Allah Ackbar o'er Nevada's summit rolled.
O to see the groves of Soxa; Almeria's bowers of love;
Court of lions; myrtle gardens, and the snow-crowned peaks above;
Raise aloft the Prophet's banner! Place it on Alhambra tower!
Up, ye valiant sons of Islam, and defy Ferdinand's power!
'Tis too late! The swords are broken and the turbans torn amain,
And the flowers of Andalusia withered on España's plain;
Ali Atar, Abil Gazan, ye were lions in the fight;
Aben Hassan, Aben Farhar, stainless chief and peerless knight.
Hear the hooting of the scoffers? Give me but a thousand lance!
I will sweep them as I swept the cavaliers of Spain and France.
Blind, O God! I had forgotten they had burned Ez Zagal's eyes,
One who blanched before his falchion did the treacherous deed
   devise;
Take me hence, O gracious Allah, from this base, deceitful land,
Great Ez Zagal met his foemen eye to eye and brand to brand;
His the honesty of purpose that true chivalry ensures,
Even the Spanish Caballeros called him, "Lion of the Moors."

Originally published in *The Crescent*, November 22, 1905

The Clarion of Islam

Are the sons of Islam sleeping?
   Is the sword of Islam broke?
Must the Khalif of the Faithful
   Bow before the Christian yoke?
Is the martial power departed
   From the line of Ertoghrol?
Or the flag of Islam flying
   O'er the towers of Istambol?
Keep it flying then ye Muslims,
   Keep it in its honoured place;
Rally round, ye best and bravest,
   Of the valiant Turkish race;
Scorning death and peril and hardship
   For the name your father's won,
Every pennon, every falchion,
   Waving in the morning sun;
Right is on your side, and justice
   Soars with every flashing blade;
Marshall then each steady squadron,
   Marshall then each strong brigade;
In your veins the blood of heroes
   Coursing in a crimson tide,
They were not afraid of action,
   Will their sons the battle bide?
Where is now the fearless manhood
   That your worthy fathers knew?
Underneath the Prophet's banner
   Braver hearted never drew;
Have their scions lost the vigour
   That imbued those mighty arms
To withstand the strongest coherts,
   Revel in the war's alarms?
Silent in your mausoleums,

Wake ye silent dead! I say,
Waken from the sleep of ages!
Teach your sons to lead the fray;
Rise, I say, and teach the Muslims
How to win undying fame;
How to die for home and freedom;
How to die for Osman's name.

Originally published in *The Crescent*, December 13, 1905

To His Imperial Majesty Ghazi Abdul-Hamid Khan Sultan of Turkey, Emir-el-Mumooneen[26]

O, son of Osman, unto thee
　This book I humbly dedicate,
The glories of thy dynasty
　Its pages faithfully relate.
They tell thy noble father's deeds,
　In battle's sternest splendour clad;
Of Selim and the Bayezids,
　Of Suleyman, and great Murad.
Also of monarchs, princes, peers;
　Of Muslim knights and Muslim lords,
The flight of arrows, ring of spears,
　The musket flash, and whetted swords,
How Ertoghrol appeared in fight,
　Of Orkan's fame and courtly grace;
Of Kara-Osman's matchless might,
　The founder of thy royal race.
And how the noblest knights of France
　Went down amid the blood and stour;
And how Mohammed's conquering lance
　For ever ousted the Ceasar's power.
Let Truth arise, and 'mid the cloud
　Of prejudice attest their fame;

---

[26] See note on page 80 for information concerning Sultan Abdul Hamid II.

Let Truth arise in thunder loud,
    Uphold the great Osmanlis name.
Scion of Osman's glorious line,
Long may thy Star and Crescent shine;
Long may thy flag the tempest ride,
Tho' winds of war be circling wide;
May victory for ever grace
The sword of Osman's kingly race.
The Phoenix loves the spicy bower,
But thou, O chief, the battle stour;
Not birks where fragrant odours dwell;
But bowers of steel 'mid battle yell;
The tramp of men, the neighing steed,
The Tekbir roll, the knightly deed.
Of great Mohammed's stem a shoot,
A branch of Islam's fertile root;
A shoot of power, a branch of might,
The Conqueror's fire in thee relight;
The fire that burned when Suleyman
The trembling west with troops o'erran;
With flaunting banners, sturdy spears,
Nor Christendom produced their peers.
Those dauntless men of generous wrath,
As rivers sweep they swept their path;
E'en as the rose is first of flowers,
So they were fist of warlike powers;
E'en as the lily's cup is white,
Their shields with honour, clear and bright;
E'en as the tulips' flame is red,
The blood of foeman duteous shed,
No age but theirs produced such lords,
No other age bore nobler swords;
In ardent youth's unclouded light,
The virgin dawn compared to night;
Their strength by Khalid's soul empowered,
Their steel in combat wild deflowered;
Chieftains they were to empire wed,

No finer spears the battle led;
Valiant, magnanimous, tried and true,
The paths of time no nobler knew.
As strong as eagles winged in flight,
Their banners soared aloft in fight;
They trod the path by Allah given,
As wandering moons tread over heaven;
A path illumined by valour's ray,
As circling suns illume the day.
The night's dark veil festoon'd with stars,
Their veil a host of scimitars;
A blaze of steel, the lightning's breath;
The glare of day, oblivion, death;
Engraven deep on history's page,
Their deeds, the hope of every age.
The glories of Iconium field
Effulgent made thy fathers' shield;
The laurels that Nicopolis gave
To Ilderim, the true and brave;
As Plevna loud with pealing praise,
Like thunder of imperial days;
When Turkish banners were unfurled
In warlike pride before the world;
When thronging squadrons lightly mailed,
By heroes led, o'er foes prevailed;
When the Osmanli martial ire
Enkindled with consuming fire,
A hundred thousand throbbing breasts,
A thousand fields of tossing crests.

True son of Islam, tho' in fight
Thy banners shine, unclouded, bright;
May peace with honour be thy part
The aim of every noble heart.
Remember how the Prophet wrought,
And follow well the words he taught;
Strong for the right, but slow to wrath;

Tread Abu Bekr's earnest path.
Triumphant splendour then will grace
The generous deed of generous race;
And honours round thy throne entwine,
Enhance the glories of thy line.
An empire's treasures in thy hand
Be thou their guide and guarding hand;
Be thine the Khalif's faithful part,
And thine the true parental heart;
To rule the nation, frame the laws,
Thy people's good, their sovereign's cause;
In joy and woe, in peace and war,
Be thou their light and pilot star;
The hope of all the good and true,
The light Abdallah's offspring knew;
The light that shone on scroll of gold,
When over Hira thunder rolled,
The scroll that bore the morn of light
In vision on Al Kader night;
The night of power when joy is born
And all is peace till rosy morn.
Hail! Osman's scion, strong of arm,
To shield thy people from all harm;
The bird of time is winging fast,
Our actions live when we have past;
'Tis thine to act the kingly part,
The warm, unfettered, royal heart;
Let love unite with sovereign grace,
Thy name shall gain immortal place;
The towers wherein thy fathers sleep
Thy sons maintain and ever keep;
Salaam Emir, faithful stand,
Be truth and right thy high command.

Originally published in *The Crescent*, April 18, 1906

[Untitled]

Lift I say the flag of Islam
   Place it on the hills again,
Every beauteous fold revealing
   To the world-wide sons of men;

You remember how your fathers
   On the hill-tops of the world
Careless of all opposition
   Every spotless fold unfurled.

Let us follow their Example,
   Staunch of heart and strong of hand,
Till the sacred light of learning
   Brightens every Muslim land;

In the thunder of the conflict
   Raise the voice and wield the pen,
We shall plant the flag of Islam
   In the fields of thought again;

Even as the Lord Muhammed
   In the "Times of Ignorance,"
Touched the heart and broke the idols
   Of Arabia's pagan lance.

Then, all worthy sons of Islam,
   Gird your armour on I say,
For the morning light is dawning
   Heralding the coming day.

   Originally published in *Essays on Islamic Philosophy* (1909)

SAMUEL (SAMI) PIGEON (CA. 1860)

Sami Pigeon was an active participant in the affairs of the Liverpool Moslem Institute beginning around 1897, and he often corresponded with Sheikh Abdullah Quilliam while in Paris during 1898. He served on the Committee for the organization in 1900, lectured to the Institute's Debating Club, and attended various functions. He had many poems published in *The Crescent* between 1898-1901; however, most were non-religious in nature and not reproduced in this volume.

[Untitled]

There is none so wise,
There is none so deep,
To trace the ocean
That we seek.
E'en the wisest
They have fell,
Who can stand?
None can tell.
Where then upon the ground
Is the place of safety found?
'Tis when beneath the Crescent
We do stand,
And take the helpless poor
By the hand
When we do all fraud eschew,
And do live as Muslims true,
Oh, how different from the band
Who do at street-corners stand,
And with drum-sticks in their hand,
Shout "Blood and Jesus we demand!"

Originally published in *The Crescent* August 31, 1898

A Laudatory Ode

Blessed be the Muslims,
   Throughout all the world
Allah, in the Koran,
   His wonders hath unfurled.

There, within those pages,
   Allah plain hath told
All that man need know—
   Truths like shining gold.

Muhammed (best of prophets)
   Is Allah's prophet true;
His glorious revelation
   Brings peace to me and you.

Thanks we give to Allah
   That he to us did send
That great messenger—
   Our prophet, priest and friend.

Originally published in *The Crescent*, March 21, 1900

SHEIKH W(ILLIAM) H(ENRY) ABDULLAH QUILLIAM (1856-1932)

Sheikh William Henry Abdullah Quilliam was born in Liverpool in 1856, the son of a watchmaker. He was of Manx descent and brought up Wesleyan Methodist, but later turned to Unitarianism. After completing his education at the Liverpool Institute, he became a successful solicitor. However, he was struck ill in the early 1880s and travelled to North Africa to convalesce in a more suitable climate. During his travels he became interested in and began seriously studying Islam. In 1887, he publicly declared his conversion to Islam, gathered like-minded followers, and established the Liverpool Moslem Society and later the Liverpool Moslem Institute in 1889. His works *The Faith of Islam* (1889) and *Fanatics and Fanaticism* (1890), based on a series of his lectures, became well known in the Muslim world and translated into many languages. In 1893, he was honored as an 'alim (Islamic Scholar) by the University of Al-Qarawiyyin (Islamic University of Fez). A year later, he was named Sheikh-ul-Islam of the British Isles, head of the British Muslims, by the Turkish Sultan. In 1899, the Shah also named Quilliam the Persian Counsel in Liverpool. Quilliam was somewhat of a renaissance man: he practiced law; wrote poetry and fiction; was well versed in geology, philology, ancient history and myth, and theology of many religions; and was a member of the Liverpool Manx Society. In 1908, he was embroiled in an ethics scandal concerning his solicitor practice. This event ultimately sealed the fate of the Liverpool Muslim Institute, which rapidly declined soon after his departure to Constantinople. He spent much of the remainder of his life at his estate at Woodland Towers, Onchan, Isle of Man, but is thought to have reintegrated into British Muslim circles under various pseudonyms. Quilliam was by far the most prolific poet published in *The Crescent* and *The Islamic World*, penning well over fifty poems from 1893-1907. Besides Islamic themes, he often wrote love poems and others concerning his familial homeland, the Isle of Man.

Other sources consulted:

"A Short History of the Progress of Islam in England," *The Crescent*, January 19, 1898, p. 35-36.

Guilford, John. "Quilliam, William Henry." *Oxford Dictionary of National Biography Online*. 2004. 29 March 2005 <http://www.oxforddnb.com/view/printable/73031>.

Wolffe, John, ed., *Religion in Victorian Britain*. Vol. 5, *Culture and Empire*. Manchester: Manchester University Press, 1997, p. 247-48.

An Isha Prayer

God grant Thy servants peace,
And blessings still increase
   Upon us here.
To us Thy will unfold,
In grace us still behold;
   Our weary spirits cheer
With peaceful thoughts.

Bless us and all at home;
Protect all those who roam
   From sin and death.
Now night returns again
Let us in peace remain,
   And guard our every breath
'Til morning light.

Originally published in *The Islamic World*, May 1893

Moslem Morning Hymn

"Regularly perform the prayer at daybreak,
for the prayer is borne witness unto by angels…

And say, O Lord, cause me to enter with a
favorable entry, and cause me to come forth
with a favorable coming forth; and grant me
from Thee an assisting power."—Sura 17, Koran

Oh, Allah, for another night
   Of peaceful sleep and rest,
For all the joys of morning light,
   Be Thou forever blest.
Here on this new born day we give
   Ourselves anew to Thee;
That as Thou wishest we may live,
   And what Thou willest be.

Favor us with Thy blessing, God,
   As we this day begin;
Preserve us from all evil, Lord,
   And keep us free from sin.
Assist us by Thy mighty power;
   Thy helping aid us lend,
To serve Thee from this early hour,
   Until the day shall end.

Whate'er we do, great things or small,
   Whate'er we speak or think;
Thy glory may we seek in all,
   And from no duty shrink.
Merciful God, to Thee we pray
   Us to protect and bless,
And keep us by Thy grace alway
   In paths of righteousness.

Originally published in *The Moslem World*, May 1893

In Memoriam[27]

William Obeid-Ullah Cunliffe
Died Sunday, 24th February, 1894

"God inviteth you unto the dwelling of peace."
—Koran, Sura 10, "Jonas"

Gone from this world of sorrow,
Gone from its toils and tears,
Gone to that bright to-morrow,
To rest through endless years,

Now all his cares are ended,
Now all his labour is done,
His soul above ascended,
To receive the prize it won.

He died without even a struggle,
Or convulsive throb of the breast,
He was leaving this world of trouble,
And entering eternal rest.

The clay form that encircled his spirit,
While here on this earth he abode,
Has released the soul that did merit,
And receives now reward from God.

His name will be treasured for ever,
Wherever Islam shall be taught,
As one whose every endeavour
Was to act as a Muslim ought.

Then let each Muslim stand by each other,
And, praying to Allah so true,

---

[27] See page 19 for information concerning W(illiam) Obeid-Ullah Cunliffe.

Beseech that the seed sown by our brother
May yield a full harvest true.

That England may soon be reclaimed
From it's present bigoted creed,
And follow the teachings of Ahmed,
God's prophet in truth and in deed.

   Originally published in *The Islamic World*, March 1894

The Moslem's Refuge[28]

While slowly fade the glorious beams of light,
And round me gather now the shades of night,
While earth is wrapt in deep obscurity,
Refuge, O Lord, I only have in Thee.

When plotting men arrange their deep-laid schemes
With craft and art, unthought of e'en in dreams,
From their vile plans thus laid so cunningly,
Refuge, O Lord, I only have in Thee.

In tangled forests, wild and far from home,
In distant lands, if perchance I should roam,
When wild and furious beasts roar savagely,
Refuge, O Lord, I only have in Thee.

When storms and winds arise and tempests lower
And crashing peals of thunder show their power,
And direful lightning flashes vividly,
Refuge, O Lord, I only have in Thee.

When weakened pulse, and still more feeble breath,
Betokes the tine when o'er the bridge of death

---

[28] This poem is the 113th and 114th Suras of the Qur'an rendered into English verse.

I leave this world to meet Eternity,
Refuge, O Lord, I only have in Thee.

Originally published in *The Islamic World*, July 1894

Scale Force

"God is the creator of all things; He is the one,
the victorious God. He causeth water to descend
from heaven, and the brooks flow according to their
respective measure, and the floods bear the floating
froth."—Sura 13, "Thunder," Koran

      It falls
Within a rift between the granite walls,
On either side, the bleak cold stone
Where leafy ferns, and tender moss alone
Find resting place. Between the waving shrubs
 on high,
Calm and serene, is dimly seen the sky,
Whilst down the narrow gorge, the stream
In one long silvery thread doth seem,
In one continual glittering shower,
An avalanche of diamonds to outpour.
Beneath the fall, a cup-like bowl
Receives the stream, then onward it doth roll,
With a low rumbling, grumbling sound,
O'er ruddy boulders, now worn smooth and round
Until another smaller leap it takes,
While all around the spray, like snowy flakes,
Is scattered. And then, as though its mighty
 wrath
Had been in one angry burst poured forth,
It gently ripples through the grassy mead,
And to the distant lake doth slowly speed,
And seems as though it murmured on its road
Low cadences of hymns to Nature's God,

Whose might hand hath formed them all,
The lake, the brook, the rocks and waterfall.

Originally published in *The Islamic World*, December 1894

The Triumph of Truth

> "Truth is come, and falsehood is vanished, and
> shall not return any more."—Sura 34, "Saba," Koran

The thrones of time shall pass away,
   As Egypt, Babylon, and Tyre;
Earth's mighty cities all decay,
   And kings and conquerors expire;
But Truth shall, in eternal bloom,
   Survive, though unbelievers rage,
Shall see foul error meet its doom,
   And flourish through eternal age.

The Sun may cease to pour forth light,
   And lost may be moon's silv'ry ray,
The stars expire in endless night,
   Vanish the planets all away,
But Truth shall raise her peerless head
   Above the ruins of them all;
And smile, when time and tide are fled,
   Before the Truth falsehood shall fall.

Exultant then shall be the cry
   O'er errors throne, prostrate in dust,
And Muslims see that Good, Most High,
   In whom they always put their trust,
Bid Truth commence its endless reign,
   Falsehood vanquish'd and triumph'd o'er,
The "True direction" made most plain,
   And error to return no more.

22nd December, 1894

Originally published in *The Islamic World*, January 1895

The Lessons of Experience

How bright the untried future seemed,
When years ago I sat and dreamed,
  In youth's sweet morning hours,
With not a thought of weary pain,
Which riper years bring in their train,
  To blight hope's fairest flowers.

With eager eyes, yet half afraid,
I scanned the time then just ahead;
  When joyous boyhood o'er,
School-days expired, tasks thrown aside,
My little barque borne on life's tide
  Would unknown shores explore.

Those years rolled on; I then attained
My full manhood; the heights were gained,
  Which once seemed far away;
Did hopes in full fruition lie?
No; they were only born to die—
  Frail blossoms of a day.

And I have learn'd that human life
Is one of pain, of care, and strife;
  That only now and then
Bright sunbeams o'er our path will stray
To cheer awhile our gloomy way,
  Then quickly fade again.

Yet still this lesson I've been taught,
Although I've not gain'd all I sought,
  And pride's had many a fall,

Yet to freely say, with mind unsoiled,
'Tis better to have liv'd and toiled
   Than never liv'd at all.

26th January, 1895

   Originally published in *The Crescent*, January 30, 1895

Maxims for Muslims

   "Invite men unto the way of thy Lord, by wisdom
and mild exhortation; and dispute with them in the
most condescending manner: for thy Lord well knoweth
him who strayeth from His path, and He well knoweth
those who are rightly directed."—Sura 16, "The Bee," Koran

Be not hasty in opinion;
  Slowly judge your fellow man;
Haste may hide the good dominion
  Acts of folly have outran;
What if he has erred often,
  Should we not remember still
Gentle admonitions soften
  And attract the stubborn will?
Language harsh and wanting feeling
  Bows the spirit for a time,
Rankles where the wound was healing,
  And perhaps excites to crime.
Are you free from human errors?
  Are your faults so few to scan,
That you wield a sword of terrors
  O'er your weaker fellow man?
Lift the veil from that proud spirit,
  Ask if you remember aught
Where loud censure you did merit
  Had you then been fairly caught?
Every man should guard his station,

And his failings fairly scan,
And remember that temptation
  Comes to all his fellow man.

21st March, 1895

Originally published in *The Crescent*, March 27, 1895

Circumstances Alter Cases

"Enquire not too curiously into other men's failings."—Sura 49, Koran

A rich man proudly walked along
  The straight and narrow way;
He lifted up his head in pride
  To hear the people say:
"That is a pure and honest man—
  The noblest work of God;
He's built upon a perfect plan,
  He virtue's path has trod.

"No moral law does he transgress,
  He's good and true and kind;
'Tis hard amongst the walks of man
  A purer soul to find."
'Twas thus they praised him while he lived,
  And filled his heart with pride,
And when at last his end did come,
  And like the rest he died,

The priest, above his gilded bier,
  Exalted to the skies
The soul of this proud child of wealth
  As good, and great, and wise.
And said that straight to heaven's gate
  The rich man's soul was sent;

While all the people bowed, and said
  "To paradise he went."

A poor man with his load of grief
  Went staggering down the path,
And begged of God to grant relief
  And heap not on with wrath.
With weight of many grievous fears
  He tottered o'er the road,
And called on Allah thro' his tears
  To add not to his load.

He fell upon the wayside sore,
  And yielded unto sin,
And he the law, with iron hand,
  To prison quick dragg'd in.
The cold, stern judge said, with a frown,
  "A crime thou didst commit,
And thou in bond must now be kept
  Till thou hast answered it."

Into a dungeon, dark and lone,
  The poor man straight they sent,
And chained him to the prison wall,
  And bade him there repent.
And there for years he pined away,
  No loved one by his side,
Until a fairer fortune came,
  And then the poor man died.

No prayers above his dumb, cold clay,
  The silk-clad Bishop said;
But quick they bore his form away,
  As soon as he was dead.
No tears were shed above his grave,
  No mound above it rais'd;
Neglected and despised he lived—

He died despised, unprais'd.

But had he lived 'neath brighter stars,
   Perhaps the narrow way
His feet on earth had gladly trod,
   That went so far astray.
And had the rich man felt the weight
   Of care the other bore,
He might have fallen by the way,
   As men have done before.

29th January, 1895

Originally published in *The Islamic World*, April 1895

Thoughts for Thinkers

"Wealth and children are the ornament of this
present life; but good works, which are permanent,
are better in sight of thy Lord, with respect
to the reward, and better with respect to hope."—
Sura 18, "The Cave," Koran

Oh! brethren it is well to know,
   As on celestial things you ponder,
That wealth and honours here below
   Are counted but as naught up yonder.

To adverse fortune meekly bow,
   In Allah's mercy still confide;
For, though wretched your fortune now,
   You yet in heaven may abide.

A monarch may ascend the throne
   With all desire to rule aright,
And lay the regal symbol down,
   To wear above a crown of light.

Not titled earls, nor crowned kings,
   As such, are recognised above;
Kind deeds and words and other things—
   There merit rank and perfect love.

Our good deeds are sweet thoughts sublime,
   Made manifest, and starlike shine,
Recorded there from time to time
   By angels in a book divine.

Thus time may show with glory fraught,
   Some humble, good, retiring soul;
Who wealth and honours never sought,
   The most exalted of the whole.

   Originally published in *The Crescent*, April 17, 1895

To a Child Playing with Toy Bricks

Lay the blocks on nice and even,
   Place them skillfully with care;
Then your mimic house will grow, love,
   Strong, and high and very fair.

Little Florrie's eyes are gazing
   At the walls as they uprise;
"What a lovely house, dear Henry,
   You have built," she gaily cries.

Still be patient, little builder—
   Haste will but your work undo;
If the walls fall down before you,
   Other walls have fallen too.

Older hands have oft erected
   Larger castles far than thine,

Built in hope and expectation,
   Yet they crumble and decline.

Waste no time in weeping vainly
   Over errors you have made.
Work again and build still stronger,
   Some day you will be repaid.

Originally published in *The Islamic World*, May 1895

Which of Them Was Neighbour Unto Her?

> "Alas! for the rarity
> Of Christian charity
>   Under the sun."
>   *Hood*—"The Bridge of Sighs"

I saw a woman beg in the street
On the Christmas day, for bread to eat;
And loud the church-bells were chiming then,
The refrain of "Peace and Goodwill to men."

I saw a Christian, sleek and well-fed,
Pass the woman and turn his head;
The crumbs that under his table fell
That day, would have fed the beggar well.

Following the Christian churchman came
A woman whose brow was stamp'd with shame;
Out from her purse, a coin she cast,
And the beggar blest her, as she pass'd.

To the church the sleek man went his way;
The woman of shame, she blush'd to pray;
Yet which of them, the more blest will be,
Magdalene scorn'd, or proud Pharisee.

26th December, 1894

Originally published in *The Crescent*, May 1, 1895

True Pleasures

How sweet to rove at opening day,
   When May's choice flow'rs are springing;
To feel the morning's early ray,
   And hear the warblers singing.

How sweet to rest in shady grove,
   When summer sun is shining;
And watch within the gay alcove,
   The tendrils gently twining.

Those happy moments, Oh! how sweet,
   When true love's vows are plighted;
And all the hopes and wishes meet,
   In heart and soul united!

Sweet, then, is the responsive sigh,
   From maiden's bosom stealing;
Sweet, too, the pledge and tender tie,
   The fond affection sealing.

How sweet is liberty to those
   In dungeons dark and dreary;
And sweet the hour of calm repose,
   To pilgrims weak and weary.

And Oh! how doubly sweet it be,
   The joy that follows mourning;
And, for a parent, sweet to see
   A long-lost child returning.

Sweet, too, is friendship's soothing balm,
  With tender, kind, emotion;
But sweeter far the holy calm
  Of Islamic devotion!

When fervent strains of gratitude,
  Breath'd from a heart o'erflowing,
Ascend to God, who ev'ry good
  So richly is bestowing.

To stand within the Muslim zone,
  Each brother kindly greeted,
And feel 'tis not from lips alone,
  Ul humdo is repeated.

1st May, 1895

Originally published in *The Islamic World*, June 1895

Hope On! Hope Ever!!

"Wherefore persevere with patience: for the prosperous issue shall attend the pious"—Sura 11, "Hud" Koran

Shed no tears when the dark skies frown,
  Patiently rest;
No storm the rainbow's smile can drown;
  Hope for the best!

Still there's a light somewhere; some day
  From East to West
Will shine a deathless, glorious ray—
  Hope for the best!

Old adage! Yes, but not less sweet,
  Divinely blest!
Although the sharp stones gash your feet,

Hope for the best!

What good is sighing? Time yet flies,
   Life is unrest;
Blot not the blue in Allah's skies—
   Hope for the best!

'Tis not the dross, but sterling gold
   That stands the test.
Pursue with patience, firmly hold—
   Hope for the best!

Hope on, hope ever! You will find
   Your life-long quest,
Peace for the soul, calm for the mind,
   Eternal rest.

Originally published in *The Crescent*, March 18, 1896

A Gem from Saadi[29]

"Bamedadan ki lefawt nekuned layl u nehar.
Khosh burved damens sahraa vou temasha ye behar.
Sofi ez sauxmia ger Khaima bezed ber gubzar.
Kin ne vakt est ki der Khané nishinee beekar."
                                      -Saadi

When night and day in length are equal,
   And the grass springs from the sod,
From admiring Nature comes the sequel
   Of admiring Nature's God.

This is no time for mourning,
   Come out in the sunlight,

---

[29] Muslih al-Din Sa'adi Shirazi (1213?-1292) was a prominent medieval Persian poet who travelled the Islamic World in the wake of the Mongol invasion.

And humbly God adoring,
  In all His works delight.

Originally published in *The Crescent*, April 8, 1896

A Muslim Prayer

Oh, Allah! lead me onward,
  Nor let my footsteps fall,
While marching to the graveside,
  That waiteth there for all.
Smooth Thou the rugged pathway,
  That leads towards the goal,
To which each pious Muslim
  Directs his heart and soul.
Protect me when in danger,
  In sorrow comfort give,
Al-Hafiz! God preserver!
  It is by Thee we live.
And when my life be over,
  And all my race is run,
Al Jannat be my portion,
  Al Latiff, Gracious One!

24th December, 1895

Originally published in *The Crescent*, May 20, 1896

Hymn for the Prophet's Birthday[30]

The people that in darkness sat
  A glorious light have seen;
God's prophet now to them hath come—

---

[30] Note from original publication, "This Hymn is so arranged that it can be sung to 'Horsley' or any common metre tune."

Muhamed, Al Emin.

We hail thee, Allah's prophet true,
   Of prophecy the seal!
We read with reverence the book
   Thou wast sent to reveal.

For thou the burden did'st remove,
   Idolatry's fell rod;
And in thy day the idols fell
   Before the sword of God.

To bless Arabia and the world
   Most surely thou wast raised:
We'll sing thy praises evermore,
   Our Mustapha, the praised.

We watch with gentle, fostering care
   The seed that thou hast sown;
And trust to hear the world declare
   God's prophet as its own.

We laugh with scorn at those who say
   That God has had a son;
With confidence we do declare
   "La Allah," God is One.

1st Rabia-al-awal, 1314

Originally published in *The Crescent*, August 12, 1896

Waiting

"O True-Believers, be patient, and strive to excel in patience, and be constant-minded, and fear God, that ye may be happy."—Ayat 200 of Sura 3, "The Family of Imram

"Whoso doeth evil shall be rewarded for it; and
shall not find any patron or helper other than God;
but whoso doeth good works, whether such a one be
male or female, and is a True-Believer, that one
shall be admitted into Paradise, and shall not in the
least be unjustly dealt with."—Sura 4 "Women"

"Work as ye will, God will behold your work"—
Sura 9

I can wait until the harvest,
   I can wait until the dawn;
I have sown, and with the reaper
   I can wait to claim my own.

I can wait, and still be sowing,
   In due season I shall reap;
If I neither fail nor falter,
   God His promises will keep.

I can wait, for I am resting,
   In a perfect promise true,
Made by Him who is Eternal,
   Each shall yet receive his due.

Be it soon, or be it later,
   Harvest sure will come in time:
Come like showers of rain descending
   In the thirsty summer time.

Why then should the arms grow weary,
   Why the heart despairing cry?
Though the clouds look dark and dreary,
   Yet the sun is in the sky.

Darkness lasts but for a season,
  'Tis dispelled by morning ray;
After winter, summer season,
  After death, Eternal Day.

1st January, 1897

Originally published in *The Crescent*, January 13, 1897

The Key to Happiness

"The man who is not kind to others need not expect God to be kind to him."—Saying of the Prophet Mahomed

Sweet is the light of a friendly face;
  Pleasant the ripples of guileless glee.
Why should we miss e'en a glance of grace,
    One to the other, where'er we be?
      Why should we draw from a bitter spring,
      Words that we speak or songs that we sing?

Trouble and sorrow are always near;
  Failure and conflict make life look dark,
True—but the sigh of a friend sincere
    Soundeth as sweet as the song of the lark.
      Solace for sorrow, or smile to smile;
      Love maketh harmony all the while!

Think then for others, 'tis always best;
  Sweeten the cup that we all must drink;
Bite out your tongue ere you launch the jest,
    Cruel as murder to hearts that shrink:
      Cut off your hand ere you deal a blow,
      Cowardly base, on a fallen foe.

Let not the flicker of wanton play
  Steal from the glow of the hearth at home;
Think not it weak to be drawn away,
  Led by a child when she murmurs, Come!
   Man! be assured, when the loves God-given,
   Pluck at your sleeve—you are watched by
      heaven!

Treasure the heart that of old you won,
  Goodlier treasure than hoards of gold:
If you lose Love, your are all undone;
  Deadliest death is a life grown cold!
   Love is the key to the heavenly door;
Man! will you lose it for evermore?

   Originally published in *The Crescent*, March 24, 1897

The True Easter

"The pious who believe in the mysteries of faith,
who observe the appointed times of prayer, and
distribute alms out of what We have bestowed on
them; and who believe in that revelation which hath
been sent down unto thee (O Mohamed!), and that
which hath been sent down to the prophets before
thee, and have a firm assurance in the life to come:
these are directed by their Lord, and they shall prosper."—
Koran, Sura 2, verse 2.

"Be constant in prayer, and give alms; and what
good ye have sent before for your souls, ye shall find
it with God; surely Allah seeth that which ye do."—
Koran, Sura 2, verse 110.

"When a man dies his fellow-creatures ask, How much
wealth has he left behind him; but the angels inquire,
How many good deeds has he sent before him."—Traditional

saying of the Prophet Mohamed.

From one's mere self, to rise above
   All hate and lust and pride,
To soar aloft, like winged dove,
   With faith, whate'er betide.

This is the resurrection time—
   Not Easter morn alone,
But every day, striving anew
   More perfect to have grown.

Thus shall the soul find perfect peace—
   Al Jannat! blest abode!
Where cares and troubles all do cease,
   Lost is the weary load.

So may all Muslims rise each day,
   In goodness, truth and love;
From worldly troubles pass away
   To lasting bliss above.

And when their eyes are clos'd in death,
   And men count worldly store,
May angels chant, with fragrant breath,
   Their good deeds sent before.

12th April, 1897

Originally published in *The Crescent*, April 14, 1897

A Janaaza Ode to the Muslim Warriors Who Fell in the Greco-Turkish War [31]

Gather the sacred dust,
  Of warriors true and bold,
Who bore the flag of a nation's trust,
Who fell in a cause victorious, just,
  And died like heroes of old.

Gather them one and all—
  From Redif to Beyler Bey;
Come they from cottage or palace hall,
They fell for Islam, for them shall fall
  The tears of Muslims alway.

Gather the corpses strewn
  O'er many a battle plain;
From many a grave that lies so lone,
Without a name, aye without a stone—
  Gather the noble slain.

We care not whence they came—
  For dear is their lifeless clay—
Whether unknown, or known to fame,
Their cause and faith were all the same,
  They died—Muslims all were they.

Where'er the brave have died—
  Though their dust may sleep apart,
Living they struggled side by side;

---

[31] A contemporary poem memorializing the Ottoman soldiers who died in the Greco-Turkish War of 1897 (Thirty Days War), fought over the Ottoman province of Crete. The poem was written a few days after the humiliating Greek withdrawal from Crete under European pressure. An armistice led to a peace treaty that made Crete as an international protectorate, forced Greece to pay reparations, and ceded part of Thessaly to Turkey.

And e'en grim death cannot divide
   The Muslim true heart from heart.

Gather their sacred clay,
   Wheresoever it may rest—
Where they fought in the bloody fray,
Where they fell on the battle day,
   Be it East or be it West.

The *Giaour* need not dread
   This gathering of the brave;
They march but with a soundless tread,
'Tis the shades of the deathless dead
   Who come from each noble grave.

Your tears they do not crave,
   Their souls in Paradise rest;
Their dull, cold bodies may sleep in the grave,
But never will fade the fame of the brave
   Who fought for the truth with zest.

They live, they are not dead;
   'Tis only the living weep;
The men who were by Edhem led,
And the hearts that together bled,
   Together now calmly sleep.

23rd May, 1897

   Originally published in *The Crescent*, May 26, 1897

The Muslim's Evening Prayer

O Thou who gavest life, who causeth death,
Watch o'er me now I lay me down to sleep;
My body rest, renew, as Thou hast saith
Thou wilt for those who Thy commandments keep!

Let no thought of the morrow cause me pain,
Nor fearsome dreams disturb nocturnal rest;
So health and vigour renew'd I may gain
To work for Thee as Thou may deem it best;
If be for me that earth no more shall be,
And that the thread of life for me has run,
I bow my head to Thy Divine decree,
And trust my deeds Thy fav'ring glance have won.
Whate'er betides, in peace I lay me down to rest,
Resign'd to fate, because, Allah, Thou knowest best.

Peel, 26th September, 1897

Originally published in *The Crescent*, October 6, 1897

"Oh Death! Where Is Thy Sting?"

Why should one fear the approach of death?
Is it not mere cessation of breath?
Is this life all we live for? Is't the end
Of all our hopes to which our footsteps tend?
If so, then drink and bid dull sorrow fly;
Let's merry be, to-morrow we must die.
Virtue is folly, pleasure is the game:
Why should we care? In death we're all the same.
A fig for wisdom! 'tis but a foolish name:
An empty bubble that which men call fame.
To-day is ours, to-morrow—who can tell!
The bells may chime! Well let them ring a knell.
'Tis all the same: Death ends it all, you know;
We'll sow the wind, the reaping will be slow.
The reaping, did we say? Ah! there's the sting!
To our minds this doth the question bring
That needs must have an answer. Oh, this Death!
'Tis not thee that's fear'd; what's done, what's saith,
In Life, 'tis that which is the cause of fear,
Gives anguish to the mind, the eye a tear.

But if the actions of the past are just,
They'll soar aloft and leave the earthy dust,
From earth it came; it doth return to earth:
The spirit loos'd enjoys a second birth,
And opes its eyes upon a fairer scene,
An ever cloudless day. 'Tis so I ween.
And if 'tis so, and gone for ever care,
The face of death then is not black but fair.
Thou cometh, Death, thou cometh as a friend!
I wait for thee; God knoweth when to send.

11th February, 1898

Originally published in *The Crescent*, February 16, 1898

The Angel Message

Teach me, O Allah! Thou whom we adore;
Instruct me now from out Thy wisdom's store,
The reason why Thou, being just and good,
Permitteth evils to exist, which could
By e'en one word from Thee dispelled be.
Successful fraud, disease and misery—
These reign enthroned, while virtue stands reluctant
And watches vice oppose it with impunity:
Is this Thy justice? This Thy constant zeal
For all that tendest to the common weal?
To strengthen those who all Thy laws oppose,
Permit the meek to be crushed by their foes;
Why should'st Thou thus, over all around,
Leave Vice to triumph and Virtue confound?
O Allah! Speak! The reason to me state.
I heard a sound, it came from Heaven's gate,
And I looked up and saw an angel there;
It came and brought an answer to my prayer—
And smiling spoke the white one from above:
"Is earth a spot for heav'n-born souls to love!"

20th July, 1898

Originally published in *The Crescent*, July 27, 1898

Ode to the Memory of General Ghazi Hafiz Pasha[32]

Who died on the 19th April, 1897, a martyr's death, fighting for the holy religion of Islam against the *Giaours* (Greco-Turkish War).

Unroll his turban! Lay his sword aside!
  His fight is ended—bid the cannons cease;
'Twas Islam's banner under which he died,
  For him hath God proclaimed eternal peace!
Cover'd with scars, the fallen hero lies,
  No more to hearken to the loud alarms
Of cannon booming and the battle-cries—
  "*Allah Akbar!* Islam! Muslims to arms!

In gruesome heaps, the dying and the dead,
  The Muslim and the Christian, there are laid
On the Thessalian plain, where their tread
  On the green verdure soft impressions made.
And Hafiz Pasha lies there 'mongst the slain,
  Who on the morn was full of manly pride,
Maimed and disfigured, true! but freed from pain—
  Allah reward! for Islam 'twas he died!

Originally published in *The Crescent*, June 7, 1899

---

[32] General Ghazi Hafiz Pasha was killed at the age of 82 in the Greco-Turkish War of 1897 during the battle of Milounas Pass. He reportedly was advancing at the head of his troops on horseback when wounded twice (arm and hand), but he refused to dismount or give up command. He then received a fatal shot through the mouth and spinal cord.

A Vision of Paradise

One eve as I sat at the casement,
   And gazed out at the western sky,
I beheld there such wondrous splendour
   I felt as if heaven were nigh:
It appeared as if angel fingers
   Had thrown open the portals wide,
And given a glimpse of the glory
   Of the shore on the other side.

I thought as I gaz'd on the picture—
   The fairest that ever I'd seen—
I could see the high hills of glory
   And the lovely valleys between;
It seemed as if mounted on Borak,
   Like the Prophet of Allah I rode
And soar'd thro' the seven heavens,
   And saw where the angels abode.

I heard the sweet plashing of fountains
   As they fell in silvery spray;
I heard the sweet chanting of song-birds
   Caroling their heavenly lay:
I saw the immense verdant branches
   Of the Lote tree spread far and wide;
In their shade bask'd heavenly houris,
   While flowers grew on every side.

I saw there a great throne all golden:
   It shone with so brilliant a glare
That mine eyes grew dazed with beholding,
   So I faintly muttered a prayer.
I saw near that great throne of glory
   A form noble, tender and rare,
And my heart gave a throb of rapture,
   For I knew the Prophet was there.

It was not merely a fancy,
   This sweet sunset vision of mine,
The portals of heaven are ever
   Flung open at evening time,
That those then whose time is appointed
   May cast on one side earthly ills,
And soar to the heavenly regions
   And walk by those bright sparkling rills.

When for me then life's sunset cometh,
   And my mortal wanderings cease,
And when I do pass through those portals
   To enjoy the eternal peace,
I am sure that I shall remember
   In those regions so fair and far
My so strange yet beautiful vision
   Of those bright sunset gates ajar.

Maybe while I sat there so gazing
   At that vision of regions blest,
The freed soul of some True-Believer
   Entered into eternal rest,
Pass'd thro' those bright sunshiny portals
   Joying at his recent release,
And shouting with rapturous pleasure,
   Found sweet rest and eternal peace.

Pressing forward joying and joyous,
   Happy to receive his reward,
Well pleased that his labours did merit
   Approval from Allah, the Lord.
May such be all your, be my portion
   When on earth our labours are o'er;
May we also wing our flight yonder,
   And dwell on that heavenly shore.

Originally published in *The Crescent*, August 9, 1899

Islamic Resignation (1)

Thou only Allah giv'st me light,
'Tis Thee who makes the future bright,
Dispels the gloom of doubt away,
And heareth when to Thee I pray.

Though sore the trials of the day,
Thou hast decreed, so I obey,
And murm'ring not at Thy decree,
Allah, my all I yield to Thee.

I know this weary, anxious breast
With Thee will find eternal rest;
And knowing this, I do resign
My will, O Allah! unto Thine.

My earthly friends though few they be,
And chill the looks that fall on me,
I rest content, full well I know,
Who trusts in Thee need fear no foe.

I work, I wait, while here I live,
For the reward 'tis Thine to give,
Content to leave my future fate
With Thee, Allah, Compassionate!

Originally published in *The Crescent*, August 23, 1899

To My Son, R. Ahmed Quilliam Bey, on the 19th Anniversary of His Birthday[33]

My son, another year has fled away,
   And scarce a cloud obscur'd the azure sky
Of infancy and youth, scarcely a day
   But joy hath strewn bright flowers to greet thine eye.

For thou hast had thy parents' watchful love,
   And patient guardianship and tender care;
My son, no love in after years can prove
   So pure and true as such as children share.

The world to thee is yet unknown, and thou,
   Like all young men, art full of hope and joy;
May e'er thy future be as bright as now
   With happiness which time can never cloy.

I do not pray that thou throughout thy life
   May never know the weight of care and grief;
Each man who passes through the world's hard strife
   From troubles ne'er can find complete relief.

And well it is so. Thus our eyes can see
   The vanities of earth, and thus discern
The path of happiness and peace, and we
   To pure and all-enduring joys may turn.

Trust not the world: its acts deceitful are,
   And seek not all its pleasures to explore;
A canker worm doth worldly pleasures mar,

---

[33] Sheikzade R. (Robert) Ahmed Quilliam Bey was the eldest son of Sheikh Abdullah Quilliam. He was given the title Bey during an 1891 visit to Constantinople, and he appeared to be the heir apparent to the Sheikh. Ahmed took on many leadership roles in the Institute and became a key connection between the Liverpool Muslims and the Sultan of Turkey. He was later named the Ottoman Consul General at Liverpool.

True happiness it hath not in its store.

These thoughts, mayhap, you think are sad to breathe
   To you upon what is your natal day,
When all your friends their festive garlands wreathe
   Their wishes for you—all that's bright and gay;

But I well know that grief can reach the heart
   E'en when the sun of youth shines bright and clear;
A cloud may come, and all our smiles depart,
   And we are robbed of all we hold most dear.

It may hap so to thee; but earnestly
   I pray Allah to save thee from such woe,
And cause all comforts to be showered on thee,
   With all the joys that true affections know.

Thy lot on earth, my son, I pray may be
   Bless'd with contentment, calm with peace and health;
And friends trusted and tried I wish for thee—
   Better by far than luxury or wealth.

That o'er life's sea that thou may'st sail in peace,
   Thy actions such that none can say thee fie;
And when at last thy soul shall find release,
   In certain hope and trust then thou may'st die;

Secure in knowing, though thy life be o'er,
   So far as this world and its cares betide,
That sin and grief are gone for evermore,
   And peace and joy eternally abide.

1st September, 1899

Originally published in *The Crescent*, September 6, 1899

The Death of Abdullahi[34]

        Fierce the battle raged,
A hail of bullets, from the murderous Maxim gun,
Fell all around, and swept the field.
        Brave sons of Islam
From the burning sands of the Soudan
Rushed forward, fighting for
Their fatherland and faith,
Only to meet a bloody death,
And earn a martyr's crown.
In the thickest of the fray,
Where danger was the greatest,
And the fiery hail fell fastest,
Rode Abdullahi-bin-Sayed Mohammed,
Whom men had called the Khalifa.
At his right hand his bold lieutenant,
Ahmed Fedil, rode;
And many a gallant emir
Swelled the martial train.
If human bravery ere deserved
A victory to gain, that day should
Victor's laurels rest upon the brow
Of the untamable son of the Soudan;
But Allah willed it not.
Under the pitiless iron hail,
Son after son of the desert sank,
Never to rise again.
But fifty-three gallant warriors,
The flower of Muslim chivalry,
The bravest of the very brave,
At last were left to contend

---

[34] Abdullahi ibn Muhammad was named Khalifa of the Mahdist state in Sudan upon the death of the Mahdi (Muhammad Ahmad) in 1885. He continued the Mahdi's expansionist campaigns into Egypt and surrounding regions and fought against the British reconquest of Sudan. On November 24, 1899, Abdullahi died at the Battle of Umm Diwaykarat.

'Gainst iron guns which vomited death,
And hellish-smelling flames and smoke.
Further resistance 'twas in vain.
"Now yield ye, Abdullahi!"
Came the cry from the invading force.
"I yield to God alone," replied the warrior chief;
Then turned he unto the dark-skinned Youssuff,
And said, "Bring hither unto me
The white sheep-skin on which
My predecessor sat." 'Twas brought,
And straightway from off his Arab steed
Abdullahi leapt, and in a voice of stern command
Addressed his warriors thus:—
        "Oh, noble Emirs!
'Tis great Allah's will we die,
Then let us meet our death as Muslims."
So saying he sat down the sheepskin rug upon,
And gathered round him sat his bodyguard.
        Again the cannon roared,
And belched forth its tongue of flame.
Down, down they all sank to the ground;
Death had claimed them for its own:
Abdullahi shot through head, heart, arm and leg,
And all his faithful emirs perished.
'Twas thus that Abdullahi died.

Liverpool, December 10, 1899

Originally published in *The Crescent*, December 13, 1899

The Last Journey

When the clouds are dark and dreary
  At the close of mortal way;
When with falt'ring footsteps weary
  I am going home to stay—
  Evermore to stay.

Then I think of lov'd ones parted
  From me now full many a day,
And I fell quite blythe-hearted,
  I am going home to stay—
  Evermore to stay.

Absence makes the heart grow fonder,
  At least so the poets say;
And there'll be no parting yonder
  I am going home to stay—
  Evermore to stay.

Though alone the path I travel,
  Though my mortal powers decay,
My feet tread upon sure gravel,
  I am going home to stay—
  Evermore to stay.

Be it late, or be it early,
  Comes the call I must obey;
Cheerfully I'll meet it, fairly,
  I am going home to stay—
  Evermore to stay.

Originally published in *The Crescent*, December 20, 1899

Night Thoughts

Have you ever awaked from slumber
  In your bed as you lay at night,
And noticed the stars without number,
  How they shed their silvery light?
The deep stillness you bewildered,
  You felt how vast was the space,
And wondered as you considered
  Of the Power that gave them their place.

Perhaps, as you thus lay gazing
   Up at the star-spangled sky,
To add to your deep amazing
   An aerolite darted by.
Could it be that an angel zealous,
   Had seen an intruder near,
And, of heaven's sanctity jealous,
   Had thrown from those regions clear

A flaming dart at the *giaour*,
   Warning him from there to flee,
Demonstrating thus the power
   Of the Mighty One there be
Who placed those lamps so resplendent,
   Who caused to blaze as a sun
Those stars with their light transcendent?
   La'Allah Ill'allah, the One!

Originally published in *The Crescent*, July 18, 1900

Our Departed Friends[35]

We have passed the noonday summit,
   We have left the noonday heat,
And down the hillside slowly
   Descend our wearied feet.
Yet the evening air is balmy,
   And the evening shadows sweet.

Our summer's latest roses
   Lay withered long ago;
And e'en the flowers of autumn

---

[35] This poem was untitled, but recited during his lecture "Our Departed Friends." It was a memorial for Thomas Ridpath and Fatima E. Cates, two members of Quilliam's congregation who died on the same day.

Scarce keep their mellowed glow.
Yet a peaceful season woos us,
   Ere the time of storms and snow,

Like the tender twilight weather
   When the toil of day is done;
And we feel the bliss of quiet
   Our constant hearts have won,—
When the vesper planet blushes,
   Kissed by the dying sun.

So falls that tranquil season,
   Dew-like, on soul and sight,
Faith's silvery star-rise blended
   With memory's sunset light,
Wherein life pauses softly
   Along the verge of night.

'Tis so our sister yielded
   The breath of mortal life;
'Tis so she ceased the struggle
   Of this fierce worldly strife;
And saying, "it is over,"
   She winged her spirit flight.

Originally published in *The Crescent*, November 7, 1900

A Plea in Abatement

I'm foolish, you think, when sometimes you see
   I give to a child a copper or so,
When there in the street barefooted he be,
   And beggeth for alms as past him I go.

Well, perhaps you are right and I am wrong,
   Perhaps I am foolish, tender and weak;
But, still, I can't help, as I pass along,

    To feel for the poor more than I can speak.

And there's something within that tells to me
    In accents quite plain, so strong and so clear,
That an action well meant wrong cannot be
    If done with intent to comfort and cheer.

What though "those beggars are most of them bad"?
    What though their whining is part of a plan?
Still I'll be foolish and follow my "fad,"
    And help and assist them all that I can.

10th Ramazan, 1318 (1st January, 1901)

    Originally published in *The Crescent*, January 2, 1901

Ode to Scandal-Mongers

Ye folks who are fond now of jangle,
    And gloat over your neighbours' misdeeds,
And love reputations to mangle,
    And point out that flowers are "but weeds,"

I pray you to pause in your chatter,
    And to seriously think of that place,
Where folks who can scandal and flatter,
    Will be met with a pleasing grimace.

The hell where the fiend in his glories
    Sits staring at stones and at putty,
And listens to slanders and stories,
    And some of them p'raps rather smutty.

For 'tis there, most welcome, you'll enter,
    For sure 'tis appropriate to dwell
In that place, of heat the true centre,
    Those who have made of this earth a hell.

3rd March, 1901

Originally published in *The Crescent*, March 6, 1901

The Death of the Old Year

Wan, feeble and old,
Through the dismal cold,
   Slowly he tottered by,
As rang from the bell
A funeral knell,
To the world to tell
   His end was drawing nigh.

On our room that night,
With its fire so bright,
   He gazed, then turned aside;
Then with dimming eye,
But without a sigh,
He utter'd good-bye,
   And so the Old Year died.

Yes! such was the end
Of our dear old friend;
   Such the way he did die;
He cheerfully went,
For a life well spent
Brings ever content
   That no one can deny.

In good earnest strife
He had spent his life,
   His mission to fulfil;
And with conscious pride
Then he calmly died,
When God did decide

His active pulse to still.

His death was not vain
If from it we gain
   A lesson good and true;
'Tis to do our part
With both head and heart,
That when we depart
   We've nothing left to rue.

Originally published in *The Crescent*, April 3, 1901

A Muslim Hymn

Oh, Allah, to us ever dear!
   We seek to guide our souls aright;
For us there is no cause for fear
   If we do walk in Islam's light.

Thou doth protect, and Thou doth bless,
   And Thou doth consolation send
To those who do their faults confess,
   And earnest seek their ways to mend.

6th April, 1901

Originally published in *The Crescent*, April 10, 1901

A Muslim Anthem[36]

   God bless the Muslim cause:
Bless all who keep Thy laws
   And do the right.
Uphold the Muslim band,
In this and every land;

---

[36] Note from original publication, "Tune—'God Save the King'"

Give them full strength to stand
    Firm in the fight.

Strengthen and help the weak,
And teach us all to speak,
    Thy truth abound.
May love and liberty,
Truth and sweet purity,
With plenteous charity,
    In us be found.

Hear Thou the orphan's cry,
Assuage the widow's sigh,
    The foolish chide.
Let vice no more abound,
But happiness be found
In every home and round
    The world so wide.

1st Muharram, 1319 (21st April, 1901)

Originally published in *The Crescent*, April 24, 1901

The Witnesses

Yon gleaming stars, which yet each passing cloud
    For e'en a time their glory doth obscure,
Declare a truth eternal, clear and loud,
    And testify the same in language pure—
'Tis God, the One, the True, who made us shine;
This God is ours, and man is also thine.

The ocean, bearing on expansive breast
    The merchantmen of countries near and far,
Now toss'd with angry waves, now calm at rest,
    Echoes the answer back unto the star—
'Tis God, the One, the True, who made me roll;

The God, O man, of thy immortal soul

These are not touch'd by petty deeds of men,
   They are not blurr'd with his deceiving breath,
They shone and roll'd ere he was born, and then
   Shine on and roll when he is spent in death.
'Tis God, the One, for whom they roll'd and shone;
O man accept thou then this God alone!

St. Catherine's, Onchan, Isle of Man, 5th August, 1901

   Originally published in *The Crescent*, August 7, 1901

The Gateway of the Grave

The grave is deep and silent,
   Its secret is its own;
It veils in sombre silence
   A land to us unknown.

The warbling of the song-birds,
   The sunshine all around,
The busy hum of commerce—
   The grave heeds not their sound.

The widow and the orphan,
   Whose tears fall down like rain,
Stand over it lamenting;
   Their cries are all in vain!

The grave, still cold and silent,
   Within its breast of clay
Still grimly holds its secret
   Until the judgment day.

Yet from no source so surely
   Doth peace and comfort rise;
Only through its dark pathway
   March we to Paradise.

The weary soul, so anxious,
   With grief and toil opprest,
Finds peace within its portals,
   And sweet, eternal rest.

St. Catherine's, Onchan, Isle of Man, 31st August, 1901

Originally published in *The Crescent*, September 11, 1901

Some Good Advice to Single Men

Oh ye who want caressing,
   When ye are full of care
When woeful pain oppressing
   Reduce you to despair,
And you require some cheering
   Upon the round of life,
Why do you stand a-fearing?
   The remedy's a wife!

You'll find your woe and sorrow
   Will vanish in a trice;
Then why wait till to-morrow
   From wedded bliss so nice.
He lives a lonely stranger,
   A miserable thing,
Who fears there lurks a danger
   Within the wedding-ring.

He never hears the praises,
   He never knows true love,
Nor feels the fond embraces

   Like manna from above.
He dies with ne'er a tear
   Sympathetic, then shed o'er him,
And round his lonely bier
   No loving ones deplore him.

So, men, just take this schooling,
   I speak it not in jest,
Cease now at once your fooling,
   For married life's the best.
And if you'd end your trouble,
   And lead an easy life,
From single change to double,
   Take to yourself a wife!

Originally published in *The Crescent*, November 12, 1902

In Memoriam[37]

   Bro. Jemal-ud-deen Bokhari Jeffery

Yes, now he's gone, the dear old man,
   Our faithful friend is dead,
His manly heart is now at rest,
   His soul has heav'nward fled.

He sojourn'd here, through hope and fear,
   For seventy years and three,
It will be strange indeed to us
   His face no more to see.

But though we mourn, we do not rave,
   Nor fret, nor yet despond,
For though his body's in the grave,

---

[37] See note on page 73 for information concerning Jemal-ud-deen Bokhari Jeffery.

His soul has gone beyond.

13th Jomada-as-sani, 1321

Originally published in *The Crescent*, September 9, 1903

A B C (All Best Come)

Away anger,
  Always astray,
Let peace descend,
  Abide and stay.

Begone baseness,
  By baseness born,
Let truth instead
  Now sound its horn.

Contentment come,
  Come Cupid coy,
And light the torch
  Of love and joy.

Depart deceit,
  Depart despair,
Sweet peace now come,
  Begone dull care.

Exit envy,
  Erst evil elf,
Love hath no place
  For grasping self.

Foul falsehood fly,
  Fell foulness flee,
No place in heav'n
  Is there for thee.

Go grumbling growls,
   Go greedy gold,
'Tis loving souls
   Who ne'er grow old.

Honour, haste home,
   Honesty hail,
True virtue's power
   Can never fail.

Impertinence,
   Irksome, ill-born,
Ignobly fly,
   Foul, fell, forlorn.

Jealous justice
   Joyfully join
With mercy tender,
   That sterling coin.

Kindliness keep,
   Bickerings cease,
The kindly word
   E'er makes for peace.

Let lealsome love
   Lighten labour,
Selfish not be,
   Help your neighbour.

May misery
   Merge into mirth,
Malice depart,
   Slain in its birth.

Needless nonsense
  Never nourish;
Naught that's foolish
  E'er should flourish.

O'er odious
  Ostentation
Open out just
  Indignation.

Peace, perfect peace,
  Peerlessly prize,
Poor pompous pride
  Always despise.

Quarrelsomeness
  Quickly thou quit,
Bear and forebear
  Is maxim fit.

Richest reward
  Rightdoing rends;
Remember God
  The blessing sends.

Selfishness shun,
  Sweet temper shine,
Sly secret sin
  Never be thine.

Temperance true
  Try, taste and test,
'Twill prove to you
  Of friends the best.

Unjust upbraid;
  Unite to heed

Unfortunates,
   Who pity need.

Victorious
   Vanquish vile vice;
Vow villainy
   Thee ne'er entice.

Who wishes weal
   Will wisely walk,
Will work and wait,
   With wise men talk.

eXample show,
   eXceed, eXcel,
eXpect reward
   Who doeth well.

Yarely yearn
   In youthful days,
Your good deeds may
   Yank yarn of praise.

Zealot not be,
   Nor zany vain,
With zeal and zest
   Zenith attain.

   Originally published in *The Crescent*, August 10, 1904

The Riddle of Life

Birth, life and death, three potent words,
   What is it that they spell?
Our entrance in, our life upon,
   Our exit and our knell.

Is that, then, all that is compris'd
   Within those words so said?
And doth the span of passing scene
   Cry "Finish'd" when we're dead?

If such be all, alas for us!
   Poor creatures of an hour,
That bloom unseen, that die forgot,
   Like passing of a shower.

Our days but few, our cares so great,
   And pass'd in toil and strife;
Our life a span, under a ban—
   No blessing, then, is life

But if the moment of our birth—
   As we believe it be—
Is not just entrance upon earth,
   But immortality;

Then toil and care and meagre fare,
   While on the earth we stand,
Is but precursor, but the path
   That leads to other land.

Then sound of knell doth only tell
   Of life begun for aye—
That perfect life, sans care and strife,
   In the eternal day.

October 16, 1904

   Originally published in *The Crescent*, October 19, 1904

Nil Desperandum!

Courage, brother! do not falter,
  Dry your tears and cease from sighing;
Though clouds look black, they soon may alter,
  And the sun will send them flying.

"Out of evil oft cometh good,"
  Is a maxim to my liking,
The blacksmith well the iron beateth,
  But 'tis better for his striking.

Work to-day and give up grieving,
  Know that joy is born of sorrow,
And though to-day is rainy weather,
  Hap 'twill brighter be to-morrow.

Grumbling doth not make our labour
  The least bit more a pleasant task,
'Tis joyful heart that lightens trouble,
  Contentment brings to those who ask.

First the childhood, then the manhood,
  First the task and then the story,
'Tis after nightfall comes the dawning,
  First the shade and then the glory.

Woodland Towers, Onchan, Isle of Man,
  23rd October, 1904

  Originally published in *The Crescent*, November 2, 1904

Islamic Resignation (2)

I have no wish, oh Allah, but Thy will;
I have no chart but thy unerring word
Which in the cave Thy Holy Prophet heard

That blessed night upon bleak Hira's hill.
I trust in Thee, I wait in patience still
For the reward for all that I have wrought,
For good deeds done, for battles grimly fought
'Gainst passions might and all the hosts of ill.
My inmost heart, my very thoughts are known;
There is no secret hidden, unconfess'd,
For Thou dost seach, Oh Allah, every breast,
That power is Thine, and only Thine alone.
So let me live, Oh God, so let my life be passed,
That when I die, I rest with Thee at last.

10 Shaahan, 1323

Originally published in *The Crescent*, October 11, 1905

Ode to "The Autocrat of all the Russias"

Tremble now, oh mighty Czar,
"Autocrat" although you are,
Hid in corner, sound and tight,
In "a devil of a fright."
Tremble now, oh great Czar Nick,
As to power you try to stick;
Rule for you won't last much more,
Czardom's reign is nearly o'er.
List, ye Czar of "Russias all,"
Hark! the sound of Freedom's call,
Chanting in triumphant staves,
"Perish tyrants! Perish knaves!"
List! the sound now draweth near,
Chant for tyrants grim to fear;
Knell it is of despot's sway,
Harbinger of brighter day.
Day of Freedom, bright and clear,
Day that tyrants well may fear,
Day they fall, undone, unwrung,

Unwept, unhonoured, and unsung.

Originally published in *The Crescent*, December 6, 1905

Kindliness

> "Your smiling good-naturedly in your brother's face
> is charity"—Muhammad

As fair as the morning,
   And as full of grace,
Is the bright friendly smile
   On a good-natured face

As firm as a mountain,
   Deny it who can,
Is the grasp of the hand,
   Of the good-hearted man

As welcome as sunshine,
   True warmth to impart,
Is the sweet kindly word
   From a good natured heart

As pure as the dew-drop,
   So tender, so dear,
Is the sympathy shown
   By the good-natured tear

Woodland Towers, Onchan, Isle of Man,
   6 Ramazan, 1324 (22nd October, 1906)

Originally published in *The Crescent*, October 24, 1906

The Onward Path

"They who fear Allah, and strive to do right and persevere with patience, upon these shall no fear come, and they shall attain to everlasting felicity."—Koran

Oh True Believer, let no fear of pain,
Nor friendly favour, nor menace, nor dread,
Divert thee from the path, that thou shouldst tread
To reach Al-Jannat, where thou wouldst attain;
'Tis not for thee professing Islam's name,
To rest ignoble. Though thy progress slow,
Enough if onward ever it doth show,
So that each daily step advance doth claim,
And helpeth thee to further progress still;
The way to Paradise all onward lies,
Keep Islam's path, nor e'er disheartened be;
And ever yielding to great Allah's will,
Then guidance light and peace will for thee rise,
He loveth those who persevere like thee,
And from all worldly fetters sets them free.

Liverpool, 12th Ramazan, 1324 (28th October, 1906)

Originally published in *The Crescent*, October 31, 1906

After Many Years

My own, my sweet, my darling wife,
  'Tis true that years have made
A change in thee—that 'cross thy brow
  Some lines old Time hath laid;
And in thy once bright glist'ning hair
  That cluster'd round thy head,
Some little locks just here and there,
  Now shine like silv-ry thread;
But, dearest, I love still the same,

As when thy brow was fair,
When free from thought of sorrow's name,
  Thou knewest naught of care,
And thou art still, though older grown,
  My own, my dearest love,
And will remain, ever mine own,
  Till call'd from earth, above.

Liverpool, 17th Dhulheggia, 1324 (1st February, 1907)

Originally published in *The Crescent*, February 6, 1907

What Is Life?

What is our life?
A breath, a moan, a sigh,
A laugh, a smile, a cry,
A storm, a sob, a calm,
Tumult, some joy, some harm,
An earthly moment brief
That longs for some relief
And freedom from stern strife,
Such, ever such, our life!

London, 10th Jomada-as-Sani, 1325 (21st July, 1907)

Originally published in *The Crescent*, August 7, 1907

S. AMINA RIDGWAY

A resident of Pendleton, Lancashire, S. Amina Ridgway converted to Islam after reading Sheikh Abdullah Quilliam's works and corresponding with him in 1904. She was very infrequently mentioned in *The Crescent* until 1906. Her single poem was published in August 1905.

Ismail[38]

To the wilderness driven, Ismail my son!
   God's angel will follow thy mother and thee;
Thou never can die till the blessings are won,
   God has promised for thee so full and so free.
The water all spent which Ibrahim had given,
   And scorched by the sun in the desert so drear—
In opening of mankind from father's home driven,
   What was there to hope, what was there to fear?
Sad Hagar no longer could watch him depart,
   Withdrew from his nearness high aid to implore;
So an angel pointed, the sight made her start,
   And haste for the water she saw not before.
He drank and revived, they pursued on their way,
   Year's hence finds him attain'd to manhood's estate;
The daughter of Egypt smiled sweet on his day—
   Twelve princes his sons came his heart to elate.
Ismael and Isaac laid their father to rest,
   His sojourn was over in sweet balmy sleep;
In days of their youth placed in God's high behest,
   At last scene of Ibrahim the brothers may weep.
Isaac's son Esau fair daughter won
   The tide of events renews kinship once tore!
They were Ismailites purchased Isaac's grandson
   When his brothers hateful desired him no more.

---

[38] A poetic retelling of the Qu'ranic story of Ismail (Biblical story of Ishmael). In Arabic, Abraham is Ibrahim.

And so down the ages the race multiplied
   When Muhammed came all the nations to bless,
He broke the false gods and idolatry died—
   At Caaba Islamites one God confess.

Originally published in *The Crescent*, August 16, 1905

HENRY YUTE JONES TAYLOR (H.Y.J.T.)
(1826-1906)

Henry Yute Jones Taylor was known to the Liverpool Muslims almost exclusively as H.Y.J.T. He was a well-known antiquarian, genealogist, writer of Gloucestershire local history, and frequent contributor of poems to *The Crescent* from 1895-97. Many of his poems were non-religious and not reproduced in this work. He and J. W. Hollingsworth, his friend and fellow Gloucester resident, often corresponded with the Liverpool Muslims.

To Abdul Hamid, Sultan of Turkey (1)

Old England grasps with warmth thy friendly hand,
Our loyal Inds, who bear thy name and creed,
Would draw a million swords in Turkey's need,
Whose chief thou art, and thine their ideal land
But would become a dread, seditious band,
Should England prove to thee a broken reed,
And leave thee prey o' hyperborean greed
For armed wolves to waste with sword and brand
The victim of conspiracies and lies
Thou art, with subtleties of hell at work,
Which base hypocrisy cannot disguise,
To vilify and prejudice the Turk
Vile politicians would effect poor Turkey's ruin
To make a seaboard for rapacious Bruin!

   Originally published in *The Crescent*, January 15, 1896

To Abdul Hamid, Sultan of Turkey (2)

A shriek of horror echo'd through the land,
   Armenia bled; and 'mid the smoke and flame
   Implored Europa's aid, but no help came;
They said, 'twas thy "infernal crimson'd hand"

Which urged to massacre, a miscreant band.
   And fanatics upheld those deeds to shame,
   And called the world to execrate thy name.
'Twas false. Thou art humane, benign and bland,
And mourn'd disasters thou could'st not restrain;
   Dark prejudice and hate like serpents lurk
Amid'st hypocrisy and cant refrain,
   To bid atrocity with hellish work,
Bring down her northern wolves, with shot, and shell, and dirk,
And to exterminate the unoffending Turk!

Originally published in *The Crescent*, April 1, 1896

Sonnet

Millions of human beings o'ercrowd the earth,
And blushing Nature hides her woeful face
To see the wanton propagation of the race.
Oft Nature errs; when imbeciles have birth,
Ten knaves and fools to one of honest worth:
   Dark ignorance and crime the world disgrace,
   Infanticide and lust our land debase,
And virtue's spurn'd with ribaldry and mirth.
Polygamy! How pious Christians blush
   At "Islam's blot," yet cast their eyes above,
Where baptised, shameless women nightly rush
   From cities vast to vend their tainted love.
O God! whate'er the creed, whatever flag's unfurl'd
O, give us strength to bear Thy standard through the world.

Originally published in *The Crescent*, June 17, 1896

Our Lady Chapel

Here stood an altar, richly carv'd which glowed
   With all the colours of the rainbow's rays,
   Where galaxies of dazzling tapers blaze,
Here worshippers of Christian idols crowd,
And to their priest-created goddess bowed,
   Before whose golden graven image raise
   Chants of intercession, hymns of praise,
While incense curls aloft its fragrant cloud
But hark! a tumult's heard, like distant thunder
   The frantic crowds approach, the din increases,
The rush impelled by zeal, or lust of plunder,
   And hew each trace of Marian cult in pieces
He who would paganise the House of God
Invokes Iconoclasm's avenging rod!

Originally published in *The Crescent*, June 30, 1897

AMHERST D(ANIEL) TYSSEN (1843-1930)

Amherst D. Tyssen was born into a family of nobility in 1843 in Upper Clapton, county Middlesex. He attended Merton College, Oxford, where he received his B.A., B.C.L., M.A., and ultimately D.C.L. in 1877. During his time at the college, he served as postmaster for five years and was also a member of the 1st Oxfordshire Rifle Volunteer Corp. In the late 1870s, he dabbled in the study of Theism; however, he was married in a Unitarian church in 1883, where two of his three children were also baptized. Sometime thereafter, he studied and at least nominally converted to Islam. Tyssen spent his career as a well-respected conveyancer, writing several legal works. He also published books on religion, local history, and sermons he presumably gave for his Unitarian church. Some of his more notable works include *The Birth of Islam* (1895), *The Life and Teachings of Muhammad* (1907), *Law of Charitable Bequests* (1888), and *Occasional Hymns* (1902). Later in life, Tyssen became active in the Unitarian Chapel at Banbury where he was named Trustee. Nonetheless, he remained engaged in the affairs of the British Muslim community until his death in January 1930. Many of his poems were published in *The Crescent* and *The Islamic World* from 1895-1906. Several of these were excerpted or adapted from his dramatic poem *The Birth of Islam*. He also published several Islamic-inspired poems in *Occasional Hymns*.

Other sources consulted:

Howard, Joseph Jackson. *Visitation of England and Wales*, Vol. 15. London: [n.p.], 1908.

"Obituary," *Transactions of the Unitarian Historical Society*, 1930, vol. 4, no. 4, pp. 466-467.

Tyssen, Amherst D. "The Thirty-Nine Articles of English Theism," *Theistic Review and Interpreter*, June 1881, pp. 6-14

Tyssen, Amherst D. "The Result of Ignorance," *Islamic Review*, March-April 1930, vol. 18, no. 3 & 4, p. 127.

The Caliph Ali's Hymn[39]

"Now hath the sun withdrawn his light,
  Now every friend is gone,
And on this dark and dreadful night
  I here am left alone
      Friendless and dark, I need not fear,
      I know, my God, that Thou art near.

"Mine enemies their plot have laid,
  And I perforce must wait,
For every hour their blows are stayed
  May make those blows too late.
      Their plots, their blows, I need not fear,
      I know, my God, that Thou art near.

"And now approach the murderous band,
  I hear their threatening tread,
Their cunning chief his last command
  In muttered tones has said.
      That band, that chief, I need not fear,
      I know, my God, that Thou art near.

"And now I hear their swords unsheath,
  Their work will soon be o'er,
I know the quenchless hate they breathe,
  Their hand is on the door.
      Their swords, their hate, I do not fear,
      In life, in death, Lord, Thou art near."

---

[39] 'Ali ibn Abu Talib (600-661) was the son-in-law and cousin of the Prophet Muhammad and the fourth and final "rightly guided" khalifa (ruling from 656-661). The poem describes 'Ali's impending murder by the Khajarites who had turned against him.

Originally published in *The Crescent*, January 29, 1896

Hymn on Mohammed in the Cave[40]

The prophet with one faithful friend
   In the dark cavern stood,
A thousand foemen scouring round,
   All thirsting for his blood.

"Alas, my master," spake the liege,
   "Our term of life is sped;
I hear the murd'rous bands approach,
   Intent to strike us dead."

"Be not distressed!" in accents firm,
   The prophet's voice replied;
"For God is mightier far than they,
   And God is on our side.

"Will He we live, no mortal power
   Can take our lives away;
Will He we die, to Him we pass;
   No need to feel dismay."

Oh, may we thus through life's rough voyage,
   With all its tempests cope;
Make God the Rock whereon we cast
   The anchor of our hope.

Come weal: to Him we give the praise;
   Come woe: on Him we rest;
E'en death is bliss to hearts assured
   Whate'er He sends is best.

---

[40] The Prophet Muhammad had ordered his followers to leave the persecution of Mecca for the city of Medina. On the way, he and his companion Abu Bakr spent several days hiding in a cave to avoid a band of the Quraysh (tribal leaders of Mecca) trying to intercept them.

Originally published in *The Crescent*, May 20, 1896

Hymn on the Welcome to Medina[41]

The governors of Yathreb
   They laid their maces down,
They made the Meccan exile
   The ruler of their town;
To him they came for judgment,
   In each disputed cause;
They offered him their tribute,
   They bade him frame their laws.

They swore with manly fealty
   To serve him e'en to death,
Confessing him their prophet
   With life's expiring breath.
Their very lives they perilled,
   They laboured and they fought;
For in good truth they deemed him
   By God divinely taught.

Lord grant that we, renouncing
   All selfishness and pride,
At Thy command may freely
   Cast wealth and power aside.
Attentive may we listen
   Where'er Thy voice is heard,
And life itself surrender
   Obedient to Thy word.

---

[41] In 622, the Prophet Muhammad performed his hijra (migration) to Medina where he was welcomed by the fractious tribes and asked to lead the newly converted Ansars (Muslims of Medina).

Consistent with Thy precepts
   Our journey may we trend,
Stern duty's path pursuing
   Unswerving to the end.
Thus we, like Yathreb's heroes,
   Shall brave examples be
Of worldly weal discarded
   For faithfulness to Thee.

Originally published in *The Crescent*, May 27, 1896

Hymn

   The Signs of God—Adopted from the Koran

Where'er we turn our reverent gaze,
   On fields or seas or skies,
Signs of a wise Creator's hand
   Greet our enquiring eyes.

Th'alternate change of day and night
   For labour and for rest,
The varied seasons of the year
   With corn and olives blest,

The bounteous clouds, whose pitying tears
   Refresh the soil with rain,
The winds that speed the laden bark
   Safe o'er the trackless main,

The glorious sun, whose genial beams
   From earth charm fruit and flowers,
The gentle moon, that spares to heat
   But lights our darkest hours.

The stars, that guide the nightly course
   Of ship and caravan,

All, all proclaim a gracious God,
  Who formed the world for man.

Originally published in *The Crescent*, July 8, 1896

Hymn on the Purpose of Creation

From the Koran

Oh, God has not created
  The heavens and the earth,
And all that lies between them,
  In cruel sport or mirth.
He gloats not o'er the struggles
  Of mortals here below
As ruthlessly beholding
  A gladiator's show.

We men are not His playthings,
  That live our little day
To please Him with our antics
  And then be cast away.
The winds and waves and thunder
  Give no unmeaning noise,
The sun and moon and planets,
  Are more than giant's toys.

The stars, whose softened lustre
  Bedecks the midnight sky,
Are not like sparks from corn-stalks,
  That give one gleam and die.
Oh, no, in all creation
  We see a grand design,
To train immortal spirits,
  To live a life divine.

Originally published in *The Crescent*, November 4, 1896

On Immortality

   From the Koran

Who'll bring the dead to life,
   The grave's dark prison burst?
Why, He that on the dead
   Conferred their life at first.

'Tis strange that fleeting souls
   Again to-day should wake,
But no less strange that here
   They once their sojourn make.

Behold the human form
   With strength and skill bedight,
Endowed with mind and will,
   With hearing, speech and sight.

'Tis God's o'erruling power
   Has caused with wondrous care
These mortal frames to grow
   Of water, earth and air.

Then cannot God preserve
   Alive the soul He gave,
And bear it safely through
   The crisis of the grave?

Oh, yes, our spirits draw
   Their essence from on high,
Of heavenly nature wrought,
   Too noble e'er to die.

   Originally published in *The Islamic World*, 1897

An Appeal to Christians

We call our Christian neighbours
   To worship God alone,
And place nor Christ nor Mary
   As rivals on His throne.

True, Jesus was a prophet
   Inspired to teach God's will,
And show that men no longer,
   Need Israel's law fulfil.

But God, if He had willed it,
   Could straightway have destroyed
Both him and his disciples,
   And left their places void.

And Jesus to his hearers
   Prescribed a rule divine,
Call no man Lord, but worship
   One God, your Lord and mine.

Then hold his name in honour,
   Pursue the path he trod,
Observe his worthy precepts,
   But make him not your God;

Nor list to heathen fables
   That picture him God's son,
For God was ne'er begotten,
   And He begetteth none.

When He on aught decideth,
   He saith—So let it be;
And lo! It is; for all things
   Conform to His decree.

Then all good Christian people
  Come worship God alone,
And place nor Christ nor Mary
  As rivals on His throne.

Originally published in *The Islamic World*, 1897

The Battle of Bedr[42]

Turn, turn away evil with manly respect,
  Ever strive to be first to let bitterness end;
And the man who has scathed you with hate or neglect,
  Will become in due time your most trustworthy
      friend.

When the victory's gained, and in scouring the field
  Fierce enemies captured fall into your power,
Show that all to your clemency safely may yield
  Without fear of revenge in your triumph's proud hour.

Take them home to your dwellings to earn their release,
  Let them teach to your sons their wise cunning and skill,
And learn that you fight but for freedom and peace,
  And treat fallen foemen with gen'rous goodwill.

Then preach them the faith which you feel in your heart,
  Which nerves you with courage to conquer or die,
Which bids thoughts of malice and vengeance depart,
  While forgiveness and mercy their places supply.

If your might in the battle the body has won,
  Seek with love in the home to lead captive the mind;
May they enter your door that is barred against none,

---

[42] The Battle of Badr was fought between the Muslims and the Quraysh (tribal leaders of Mecca) in 624. It was a key early battle won by the vastly outnumbered Muslims.

And in your communion true brotherhood find.

'Tis alone in defence with the sword we may smite,
  If we hope to be blessed by Great Allah above;
That each soul by its conscience be guided is right,
  And religion be spread not by force but by love.

Originally published in *The Crescent*, July 14, 1897

Hymn on the Faith of Abraham

From the Koran

We hold the faith of Abram,
  Nor Christian he, nor Jew,
Long, long e'er law or Gospel
  He preached religion true:
That men have souls immortal,
  And God's behests fulfil
So be they strive sincerely
  To learn and do His will

But later scribes enacted
  Strict rules of fasts and feasts,
And unclean meats and Sabbaths,
  And offerings to the priests;
Forbad each seventh autumn
  To sow their fields with wheat,
Forbad to wed with Gentiles,
  Or at their tables eat

The gentle son of Mary,
  Recall'd God's first commands,
Disproved the law's divineness
  By dying at its hands
He spake a beauteous gospel
  Of charity and love,

Goodwill to men around us,
   And trust in God above

Yet heathen myths invaded
   The Church which bore his name,
Three gods for one were worshipped,
   For faith profession came
His words that aimed, from priestcraft
   All simple soul to save,
Were used as tyrant's weapons
   Men's reason to enslave

Last Mecca's fervent prophet
   Old Abram's creed restored,
Renounced all human fictions,
   Took God alone for Lord,
We make his words our motto,
   And all mankind invite
To still their separate fancies
   And on our ground unite

Originally published in *The Crescent*, July 20, 1898

Hymn—Who is the Pious Moslem?

Who is the pious Moslem, Who?
   He who believes in God above,
Who scans the Universe around,
And o'er its face sees marks abound
   Of matchless wisdom, power, and love.

Who is the pious Moslem, Who?
   He who believes in man below;
Who kens his spirit shall not die,
But pass before its Judge on high,
   And reap its mead of weal or woe.

Who is the pious Moslem, Who?
  He who God's holy prophet hears,
Who lists attentive to their voice,
And bids his heart thereat rejoice,
  Their precepts and their names reveres.

Who is the pious Moslem, Who?
  He who observes the hours of prayer;
Who ev'ry day at morn and ev'n
Devoutly turns his thoughts to heav'n,
  And asks for grace to lead him there.

Who is the pious Moslem, Who?
  He who gives alms to feed the poor,
His own indulgences restrains,
To soothe the helpless orphans' pains,
  Nor turns them hungry from his door.

Who is the pious Moslem, Who?
  He who preserves his heart sincere;
Who seeks to learn and do God's will,
And honours all who so fulfil
  The duties of their stations here.

Originally published in *The Islamic World*, 1899 and *The Crescent* October 18, 1905

Hymn on the Capture of Mecca[43]

Ye gates, unfold, strong walls, fall down,
  Bow minaret and dome!
The seer, who fled with life proscribed,
  Returns as conqueror home.

---

[43] This poem recounts the bloodless recapture of Mecca by the Muslims.

Ten thousand followers swell his train,
   All armed with sword and shield,
His foes have found their forces melt,
   And now must humbly yield.

No blood he sheds, no fine exacts,
   No prince to prison sends,
Forgives, forgets all injuries past,
   Treats enemies as friends.

Oh, hence may we a lesson learn
   Sweet tempers to display,
And ne'er resent the varied wrongs
   We suffer day by day.

Tho' others call our faith a sin,
   And motives bad impute,
May we no angry word reply,
   But rest in patience mute.

So shall they see that in our hearts
   God's spirit truly lives,
And honour with unfeigned respect
   The gentle grace it gives.

Originally published in *The Crescent* October 18, 1899

Evening Hymn[44]

'Tis now the hour of evening prayer,
When mortals may rest from all earthly care,
When hearts that ache and eyes that weep,
May hope to be soothed by balmy sleep.

---

[44] Note from original publication, "Tune: 'Row, brothers, row.'"

The birds that leave at dawn their nest,
To fly far and wide on their daily quest,
Return at eve, a twitt'ring throng,
And warble to heav'n their thankful song.

Or e'er you give your minds repose,
Praise God, from Whose hand ev'ry blessing flows,
May He, in night's quiescent hours,
Refresh and renew our wearied powers.

If we this day have wronged our friends,
Now let us resolve to make just amends,
And freely from our hearts forgive,
All wrongs that we suffer while we live.

And when our ev'ning comes at last,
And life's little day shall be gone and past,
Calm may our spirits pass away,
In hopes to awake to brighter day.

Originally published in *Occasional Hymns*, 1902

The Natural Rules of Duty

They say: The cattle are sacred, none shall eat thereof. Say: Produce your witnesses, who can bear testimony that God hath forbidden this. Say: Come, I will rehearse what your Lord hath forbidden: Be not guilty of idolatry, show kindness to your parents, murder not your children, draw not near unto fornication, perform your covenants, give full measure, weigh with a just balance, and when ye pronounce judgment, observe justice.—Koran cc.vi and xvii (condensed).

Think not that God regardeth
The viands which ye eat,
And deem those only righteous

Whose mouths abstain from meat.

Behold, 'tis He provideth,
All nutrient, wholesome food,
Take then the gifts He sendeth,
And own the Donor good.

But hear what He forbiddeth:
Neglect of infant life,
Ingratitude to parents,
Unkindness tow'rds a wife.

Grasp not at power or riches,
From vice and cups abstain,
Nor seek by force or falsehood,
Your neighbor's wealth to gain.

Perform your contracts strictly,
Pay ev'ry farthing due,
See that your scales be even,
Your weights and measures true.

In giving vote or verdict,
Let justice be your aim,
So shall you make the judgment,
Of earth and heav'n the same.

The path of natural duty,
By God is reckoned right,
Fictitious rules of conduct
Are worthless in His sight.

Originally published in *Occasional Hymns*, 1902

The Prophet's Resolution

> The chiefs of Mecca, having sent
> Abu Taleb, an uncle of Moham-
> med, to inform him that if he did
> not abandon his preaching they
> would kill him and his followers, he
> answered: "O my uncle, if they
> placed the sun on my right hand,
> and the moon on my left, to force
> me to renounce my work, verily I
> would not desist therefrom until
> God made manifest His cause, or I
> perished in the attempt."

The prophet felt a mission,
To preach the word of God,
To brave all opposition,
To fear no threatened rod.

Oh, had his foes the power,
To scale the heaven's height,
And pluck from out their bower,
The orbs of day and night,

On right and left hand place them,
To bar his onward way,
Undaunted he would face them,
Nor brook an hour's delay.

Filled with determined boldness,
His steadfast heart would meet,
The moon's pale silv'ry coldness,
The sun's bright scorching heat.

On, till he saw prevailing,
The cause of God on high,

Or felt, with forces failing,
His lot ordained to die.

Oh, may such resolution,
With courage nerve us all
To bear all persecution,
Entailed by Heaven's call.

   Originally published in *Occasional Hymns*, 1902

Summer Holidays[45]

Friends, who lead laborious days,
Friends, whose zeal deserves just praise,
Welcome to the restful ways,
   Summer evenings bring!

Now's the time fresh health to gain,
Give repose to wearied frame,
Come, then, join the sacred strain,
   Grateful voices sing.

Let your thoughts to heaven turn,
Strive the grace of God to earn,
Duty's lessons ever learn
   Clearer than before.

So your holidays shall prove,
Holy days of peace and love,
Crowned with blessings from above,
   Showered in ample store.

Then to work again repair,
Nerved with strength in strain to bear,
Bravely meeting every care,

---

[45] Note from original publication, "Tune: 'Scots, wha' hae wi' Wallace bled'".

As you live or die;

And when life's full thread be spun,
Labours past and tasks all done,
Heav'nly rest awaits each one,
   Safe with God on high.

Originally published in *Occasional Hymns*, 1902

Hymn on Almsgiving from the Koran

How blest is he, whose honest toil
   Provides for all his needs,
His infant children duly trains,
   His aged parents feeds.
Whose outlay, balanced ne'er beyond
   His income's bounds to spread;
A surplus saves for those who lack
   The power to earn their bread.
The orphans of his kindred first
   Demand his earnest care,
And next the blind, or deaf and dumb,
   Or maimed his bounty share.
In rend'ring alms of fruit and corn
   He chooseth portions good;
Small merit theirs, who meanly give
   Their own rejected food.
And When with dole-fund spent he hears
   The needy's piteous call,
Tho' void his purse, his heart is full,
   He speaks kind words to all.
Oh, surely they who thus through life
   Sweet mercy's path have trod,
A recompense hereafter reap,
   Of blessings from our God.

Originally published in *The Crescent* November 8, 1905

ANONYMOUS, INITIALS, UNKNOWN PSEUDONYMS

No information is available for these poets. The poems were published in *The Crescent* or other sources noted from 1898-1908.

New Christian Anthem[46]

Sacred to the Memory of the Glorious Massacre by Christians of 15,000 Mussulmans at Omdurman.

Hark! the herald demons sing
Hark! the murderous church bells ring!
The blood-red standard is unfurled;
Mars and Moloch rule the world.
Christians shout their joyous notes,
Flying at poor Muslims' throats!
Slaughter, ruin, rapine, woe!
"Onward, Christians, onward go."

In the Temples of the Lord
Hoist the flag and wave the sword.
Let the whole infernal din
At the sound of war begin.
Glory to the Christian plan
War on earth and hate to man.
Hark! the herald demons sing—
"Hail to Mars, our god and king!"

Praise on earth the Maxim gun,
Fit weapon for "God's own son,"

---

[46] The Battle of Omdurman (September 2, 1898) pitted the British under the command of General Kitchener against the Mahdist forces of Khalifa Abdullahi ibn Muhammad. Large numbers of Mahdists were disproportionately slaughtered in this campaign, defined by modern versus traditional weaponry.

Praise on high the shrapnel shell,
To send Muslims down to—well,
Somewhere hotter than Soudan.
Glory to the Christian plan!
Hark! the yelling demons cry—
"The millennium sure is nigh!"

Originally published in *The Crescent* October 5, 1898

A Death in the Desert

Tangled beard and an old grey head,
    And a face that showeth pain;
A shrunken form, and a desert storm,
    And the stinging, sandy rain,
In a dark'ning sky, a blood red eye—
    Fearsome, frightful fell—
A stifling air, a soul's despair
    And a burning blast from hell.

Tangled beard and an old grey head,
    And a face that shows no pain;
For the desert storm had stilled that form,
    And its shroud was the sandy rain.
And the clear blue sky with its beaming eye
    Now works a magic spell.
No stifling air, no blank despair—
    He's gone where the houris dwell.

Liverpool   W.R.

Originally published in *The Crescent*, April 11, 1900

The Call to Prayer

"Allah! Hu Akbar!"

I hear a cry in the silent night,
   Ere the dawn breaks cold and grey,
It fills my soul with strange delight,
    Tho' it sounds so far away.
      Allah, Hu Akbar! Allah, Hu Akbar!
      Ye faithful, come to prayer!

I hear it again at noontide hour,
   When Nature is bright and gay,
It seems as if bird, and tree, and flow'r
   Burst forth in joy's roundelay.
      Allah, Hu Akbar! Allah, Hu Akbar!
      Ye faithful, come to prayer!

I hear it again as day declines,
   And the labourer's task is o'er!
Its echoes stir the lofty pines
   And above the city's roar.
      Allah, Hu Akbar! Allah, Hu Akbar!
      Ye faithful, come to prayer!

When the sun goes down I hear it again,
   When the weary seek their rest,
When clouds fly past, and a sound of rain
   Comes sobbing out of the west,
And, oh! it is a glorious strain
   With which my soul is blest.
      Allah, Hu Akbar! Allah, Hu Akbar!
      Ye faithful, come to prayer!

By night and day, by eve and morn,
   The call rings in mine ears
It can admonish, it can warn,

Can rouse, or calm our fears,
Allah, Hu Akbar! Allah, Hu Akbar!
   Despise the call who dare!
     Allah, Hu Akbar! Allah, Hu Akbar!
     Ye faithful, come to prayer!

Originally published in *The Crescent*, August 19, 1903

In Memoriam

The Children

Eye hath not seen nor ear heard
   What God prepares in love
For all the little children
   Who rest with Him above.

Happy and safe in Paradise,
   Free from all care and pain,
Watching in love o'er parents dear,
   Who would wish them back again?

By waters still, 'mid pastures green,
   Their hours are pass'd away,
No longer feel they this world's heat
   Or burden of the day.

Tho' few the days that some have spent
   Upon this earthly shore,
Yet God hath call'd them hence to dwell
   With Him for evermore.

For Paradise itself would not
   (Tho' beautiful and fair)
Be perfect if we found at last
   There were no children there.

From ev'ry age God gathers them,
   And white-rob'd spirits tell
Us, on our entering Heaven,
   "He doeth all things well!"

For first to greet our entrance there
   Those whom we lov'd below,
For whom in twain our hearts were riv'n
   And bitter tears did flow.

Then only to our eyes reveal'd
   Great Allah's perfect love,
When He gives us back the children
   In those bright realms above!

        Fiordelisa

Originally published in *The Crescent*, August 31, 1904

Hope

Hope is the star that guides our way,
   O'er life's tempestuous sea;
And brings us safely to that bourne,
   The haven where we would be.
'Mid busy toil and trials vast,
   Which in this world we find,
We yet can hear that '*still small voice*'
   That brings a tranquil mind.
And tho' to our dimm'd vision oft,
   The path of love is veiled,
Hope is the beacon that illumes
   Whene'er our Faith's assailed.
'Mid palaces and dungeons dim,
   However faint the ray
Of Hope entwined in every heart,
   It brings a brighter day.

And when with '*realisation*' full,
   Our hopes to us are given,
We recognise the *unseen Hand*
   Which guides our steps to Heaven!
But if on earth it is ordained
   Our hopes we should not see
Reveal'd unto our mortal eyes,
   Yet in eternity.
When Victory triumphs over Death,
   And there is no decay,
Our hopes shall bloom for ever there,
   'Mid realms of brightest day.

                Fiordelisa

Originally published in *The Crescent*, August 16, 1905

Press Onward!

Press onward in Life's battle,
   Where moral courage wins,
Your charity shall cover
   A multitude of sins,
If given in all sincerity
   To God who reigns above,
Amid that life so perfect,
   Whose attribute is Love

Press onward in the conflict,
   Give succour to the weak,
Be kind to all God's creatures,
   The Heavenly kingdom seek
So that when Satan tempts you
   To do the thing that's wrong,
Ye shall in well prov'd armour
   Be stronger than the strong

O, girls and boys of Islam!
   Your talents one or more
God gives you for His service,
   To add unto His store,
If faithful in your efforts,
   And kind to man and beast,
It may be in God's kingdom
   You will not be the least

              Fiordelisa

Originally published in *The Crescent*, April 1, 1908

Cheer Up

   Just be glad!
Oh, heart of mine we shouldn't
   Worry so!
What we've missed of calm
   we shouldn't
     Have, you know!
What we've met of stormy pain,
And of sorrow's driving rain,
We can better meet again,
    If it blow!

We have erred in that dark hour
     We have known
When the tears fell with the shower,
    All alone
Were not shine and shower blent
As the gracious Allah meant?
Let us temper our content
With his own

Originally published in *The Crescent*, April 15, 1908

POEMS FROM AMERICAN SOURCES

ST. GEORGE BEST (1860-1936)

St. George Best was a Midwestern bookseller infamously connected with the pornography trade. To that end, he was sentenced to three years in prison in 1884 for mailing obscene materials, but was later pardoned by President Grover Cleveland. He wrote poetry from at least the mid-1870s until after the turn of the century. He had poems published in periodicals such as the *Chicago Tribune, New England Magazine* (1890), *Lippincott's Magazine* (1892), *The Book-Lover* (1900), *Metropolitan Magazine* (1901), *Smart Set* (1904), and several others. Best was also a contributor of poems and articles in several Theosophical publications in the early 1890s. He had one poem published in the September 1893 issue of *The Moslem World* (New York, New York), the publication of Muslim convert and longtime Theosophist, Mohammed Alexander Russell Webb.

Other sources consulted:

Gertzman, Jay A. *Bookleggers and Smuthounds: The Trade in Erotica, 1920-1940.* Philadelphia: University of Pennsylvania Press, 1999

The Public Papers of Grover Cleveland: Twenty-second President of the United States. March 4, 1885 to March 4, 1889. Washington, D.C.: GPO, 1889.

Al Sirat

Lo! all who hope for paradise at death must pass,
  So tells the prophet, o'er the bridge of Al Sirat;
Unsurer to the footstep than the smoothest brass
  That ever Bagdad armorer polished on his mat.
And narrower likewise than the keenest cimeter

Wherewith the Muslim clove the godless infidel;
And which, the learned Muftis teach, expands, as 'twere,
   From edge to edge, above the trackless pit of hell.

More swiftly than the lightning's awful flash they speed,
   Who in their lives the Koran's truths exemplify;
And some there be that spur like the galloping steed,
   And some with the *shahin*, some with the eagle vie.

Some cross like the rider who has nothing to win,
   Footless as drunkards reel some, unstable and slow;
And millions, overcome with the weight of their sin,
Topple headlong, unwept and unpitied, below.

Live rightly, O mortal, and thine shall be fourfold
   The measure of happiness Allah decrees;
And when thou art come to Sirat, thy virtues, behold!
   Will bear thee as swift as Al Borak to ease.

Chicago, U.S.A.

Originally published in *The Moslem World*, September 1893

J. L. M. GOUGH (1875-1934)

Details of James Le Roy M. Gough of Hamilton, Ohio, are obscure. He was listed in *The Crescent* as J. Lecky McGregor and J. Le Roy MacGregor. Gough corresponded with *The Crescent* beginning in 1896. He once provided a copy of an article he wrote to his hometown newspaper signed "A Hamilton Moslem." At one point, he also requested that Sheikh Abdullah Quilliam send qualified Islamic missionaries to the United States.

The Compassionate

Moslem Morning Hymn

Soul of the Worlds! To thee we turn our gaze,
Bask in Thy smile, and worship in its rays:
Before Thee, God, how small doth seem a creed!
Lord of the Worlds! 'Tis Thee alone we need!

Teach us, O Allah, Thine own perfect way;
Al-Latif, lead us, that we may not stray;
Our erring footsteps guide Thou e'er aright,
Our Tower of Strength be Thou in our life's fight.

Compassionate and Merciful! To Thee,
Without another succour, lo, we flee:
Teach us to bend our stubborn wills to Thine;
Teach us the gold that doth in Patience shine!

King on the Day of Judgment! Lo, we bow
In adoration 'neath Thine august brow;
Yet for Thy Chosen One's, Muhammed's sake,
Deign our poor off'ring graciously to take!

Hamilton, Ohio, U.S.A., January 12, 1897

Originally published in *The Crescent*, June 2, 1897

CORA WILBURN (CA. 1831-1906)

Cora Wilburn was born around 1831, the only child of a well-to-do German Jewish family in the southern United States. After a privileged childhood, she was orphaned and fell on hard times. Wilburn began a journey of religious understanding, during which she briefly converted to Christianity before turning to spiritualism. Unmarried, she sewed for a living before becoming a well-known medium and author, writing articles and poems from the late 1850s through the 1870s on spiritualism, women's rights, and many other topics. Some of her Civil War-era poems were used to support worker's rights at the time. During the 1880s, she returned to Judaism and began writing articles and poetry in Jewish publications and speaking on similar topics at conferences. In December 1895 and again in February 1896, she wrote poems in support of Sultan Abdul Hamid II in *The Moslem World and Voice of Islam* (Ulster Park, New York), a publication of American convert to Islam, Mohammed Alexander Russell Webb.

Other sources consulted:

Braude, Ann. *Radical Spirits: Spiritualism and Women's Rights in Nineteenth Century America* (2nd ed.). Bloomington: Indiana University Press, 2001.

Halker, Clark D. *For Democracy, Workers, and God: Labor Song-poems and Labor Protest, 1865-95*. Urbana, Ill.: University of Illinois Press, 1991.

"Necrology," *American Jewish Year Book*, 1907, p. 505.

In Defence of the Right

Fierce denunciation, loud, unquestioned,
Urges on to Greed's unhallowed strife;
"Peace, good-will to men," the Ideal spoken,
While Fraud and Force enthral the actual life.

Falsehood veils its hideous front in seeming,
   Of Compassion's holy, sweet delight;
For the Christian slain, the world-wide clamor,
   Swiftly threaten War's imposing might!

But when Moslem is by Christian hunted,
   Softly silence o'er the outrage falls;
Scarce a voice from pulpit, home or rostrum,
   On the world's awakened conscience calls.

When the Jewish woman, in beholding
   Murdered husband, baby cut it twain,
Called upon the furtherance of God's justice,
   What reply did Christian nations deign?

Here and there a burst of indignation
   From some truth-vowed, solitary heart;
But the world, in Christian resignation,
   Kept in silent selfishness apart.

E'en beneath the Stars and Stripes of Freedom,
   Arrogance of narrow selfishness,
Would have hurled back to the Czar's dominion,
   Israel's children in their dire distress!

Ill beseems the fierce denunciation,—
   Others lack of mercy's urgent need;—
Those who keep their sympathies untroubled,
   Save in channels linked of race and creed!

Slander, Misconception, wilful Falsehood,
   Overhangs the world; great Freedom sleeps;
While fanatics toil with rage of plunder,
   As a whirlwind Bigotry o'ersweeps

E'en this land of boasted Freedom's vantage,
   Stand the warring sects 'gainst Truth at bay;
Dare assign all cruelties abhorrent
   To the Moslem's better heavenward way!

Marshfield Hills, Massachusetts, November 15th, 1895

   Originally published in *The Moslem World and Voice of Islam*, December 1, 1895

To His Imperial Majesty, Sultan Abdul Hamid II

Tread of gross oppression, heartless wronging,
   By world-wide hatred's voice ascribed to thee;
Thou, of the pitying heart's intensest longing,
   In Allah's place vowed merciful to be
   Unto the lowliest of humanity!

I hear the clamor of discordant voices,
   The war-cry of unreasoning bigotry;
In Truth's encircling calm my soul rejoices,
   For tardy Justice *must* awarded be,
   Where high endurance dwells with clemency.

Beneath the Crescent, present life of duty
   Unfolds by innate grace of loyalty;
For equal rights within thine Empire's beauty,
   A grateful people's love environ thee!
   Great sorrowing heart! nigh thy deliverance be.

From coarse attacks of Falsehood, meanly daring
   To gain the ear of special sympathy;
From the rapacious clutch of nations weaving
   The mocking symbols of true royalty;
   From craven foes that from Truth's search-light flee!

When cruel Russia gave imperial sanction
   To all of brutal hatred's enmity—
Where kept the Christian world its Love's expansion?
   When martyred Israel cried in agony,
   Came timely help o'er kindred land and sea?

And *they*, with "madness of the purple," sated,
   The Tyrant-Czars of modern history—
Shall never with the conquest be elated,
   That would subdue the Moslem sovereignty,
   Unto a yoke of base idolatry!

Never! for God is just; the world's heart beating
   In response to the o'ersearching Unity;
The awakened millions of soul-kindred meeting
   On the wide platform of fraternity,
   Proclaim the Light—Israel and Islam see!

A woman old, no earthly 'vantage seeking—
   Unto no worldly idols bent the knee;
In faithful homage, from a full heart speaking,
   This tribute of imperfect song to thee,
   Sends o'er the far wastes of the wintry sea!

Commander of the Faithful! Israel's daughter
   Knows the enmeshing hold of bigotry;
And dares believe, that never Christian slaughter,
   In brutal outrage was ordained by thee;
   Not *thine* the Century's scheme of tyranny!

I greet thee merciful and just! believing
   That human duty sacred is to thee;
That bowed in reverent Sorrow's mighty grieving,
   Thy great soul fronts the shafts of calumny;
   Triumphant soon o'er clamoring foes to be!

Glory of Israel's blessing 'circle thee,
With the World's Peace, proclaimed o'er land and sea!

Marshfield Hills, Massachusetts, February 5th, 1896

Originally published in *The Moslem World and Voice of Islam*, February 1, 1896

GLOSSARY

Aerolite – meteorite
Afreets – evil demons in Arab myth
Aiden – Eden
Ahmed – see Muhammad
Allah – God (Arabic)
Allahu Akbar; Allahu Ackbar; Allah Akbar; Allah! Hu Akbar – "God is great" (Arabic)
Andalu - Andalusia
Araby – Arabia
Architrave – lowest part of an entablature
Ayat – verse
Azrael – Angel of Death
Bari, Al – The Maker; one of Allah's 99 attributes
Bey – title of respect (Turkish)
Bismillah – "In the name of Allah" (Arabic)
Borak, al – winged horse that carried the Prophet Muhammad on his Night Journey
Brahmin – Hindu caste of priests
Caaba – See Kaaba
Caballeros – horsemen (Spanish)
Caliph – see Khalif
Cheiranthus – perennial plant with colorful flowers
Circe – sorceress in Greek myth
Czar – Russian ruler
Dirge – song of Mourning
Dons – Spanish gentlemen
Dree – suffer (Scottish)
Eddas – old Norse poems
Effendi – title of respect generally for officials (Turkish)
Emin, al – trustworthy (Arabic)
Emir – ruler (Arabic)
Emir-el-Mumooneen – Commander of the faithful (Arabic)
Espana; España – Spain (Spanish)
Eyries – aerie; bird nest perched high

Giaour – non-Muslims; infidel (Turkish)
Granadinos – inhabitants of Granada (Spanish)
Hadees – Hadiths; sayings and deeds of the Prophet Muhammad
Hafiz, Al – The Preserver; one of Allah's 99 attributes
Hajee – person who has completed the hajj, or pilgrimage to Mecca
Hazar, al – al azar; at random (Spanish)
Hidalgo – lowest nobleman (Spanish)
H.I.M. – His Imperial Majesty
Himalay – Himalaya mountains
Hira – cave where the Prophet Muhammad first received revelations of the Qu'ran
Houris – maidens in paradise
Iconium – region in Turkey
Idalian – mountain region in Cyprus
Ilderim - the lightning; epithet of Ottoman Sultan Bayezid I
Ind – India
Isha – the evening prayer time for Muslims
Islam, el – religion of the Muslims
Islamite – SEE Muslim
Janaaza – funeral prayer
Jannat, al – paradise
Jehovah – God in the Old Testament
Jumna – tributary of the Ganges river in India
Kaabah – Ka'aba; located in Mecca, it is the most sacred structure in Islam
Kadar, Al – Laylat al-Qadir; Night of Power, which commemorates the first revelation of the Qu'ran.
Karma – in Indian religions, the concept that actions have cause and effect
Khalif; Khalifa – leader of the Muslims
Koran; Kuran – Qu'ran; Muslim holy book
Kurayish – Quraysh; the Prophet Muhammad's tribe and rulers of Mecca
La'Allah Ill'allah; La illa ha, illa Allah – "There is no God but Allah" (Arabic)
Lapis lazuli – a semi-precious blue stone
Latiff, Al – The Subtle; one of Allah's 99 attributes

Lote tree – a tree marking the furthest boundary in heaven
Luna – moon
Mangonel – siege weapon
Manna – food miraculously sent to the Israelites in the desert
Marah – bitter well the Israelites encountered
Mahomed; Mahommed; Mahound – See Muhammad
Maxim gun – machine gun
Mecca – Islam's holiest city, located in Arabia
Medjidieh – knightly order of the Ottoman Empire
Mohammed; Mohamed – See Muhammad
Moor – Muslim rulers of Spain from North Africa
Moslem – SEE Muslim
Moslimah – Muslim woman
Mosque – Muslim place of worship
Mougol – Mughal; Indian Muslim dynasty
Muezzin – performs the Muslim call to prayer (Arabic)
Mufti – interpreter of Muslim law
Muhammad; Muhammed; Muhamed – prophet and founder of Islam
Muslim – follower of Islam
Mussulman – See Muslim
Mustapha – chosen one (Arabic); name for the Prophet Muhammad
Namaz – Muslim prayers (Persian and Indian languages)
Nevada – Andalusian mountain range
Nirvana – in Indian religions, the final place after the cycles of reincarnation have ended
Omeya – Umayyad; Muslim dynasty that ruled Spain
Orcan – wind storm
Orcus – god of the underworld in Roman myth
Oriflamme – inspiring symbol; rallying point
Osman – founder of the Ottoman Empire
Osmanli – Ottoman
Osmanieh – Ottoman knightly order
Paraclete – the Holy Spirit in Christianity
Pharisee – religious order of the Jews predominate during the lifetime of Jesus
Plevna – Bulgarian battle site between Russian and Turkish forces in 1877

Porphyry – igneous rocks with large crystals
Salaam – peace (Arabic)
Sciemter; scimetar – scimitar; curved blade sword
Seljukees – Turkish dynasty
Shaitan – Satan (Arabic)
Sheikh-ul-Islam – title bestowed upon those who are authorized to make important judgments
Sirat, al – the bridge to paradise
Sultan – ruler of a Muslim country (Arabic)
Sura – chapter of the Qur'an
Sybil – prophetess
Tekbir – saying "Allahu akbar" (Arabic)
Teuton – Germanic
Van – frontline of troops
Woden – Anglo-Saxon god of War; Odin (Norse)
Yathreb – region of Arabia where Medina resides

Further Reading on the Liverpool Muslims

Ansari, Humayun. *'The Infidel Within': Muslims in Britain since 1800*. London: Hurst & Co., 2004.

Ansari, Khizar Humayun. "The Quintessential British Muslim: Abdullah William Henry Quilliam (1856-1932)," *Arches Quarterly*, Winter 2008, vol. 2, issue 3, pp. 46-51.

Macintosh, John. *The Poets of Ayrshire from the Fourteenth Century till the Present Day*. Dumfries: Thos. Hunter & Co., 1910.

Murad, Abdal Hakim. *Muslim Songs of the British Isles*. London: Quilliam Press, 2005.

Parkinson, J. Yehya-en-Nasr. *Essays on Islamic Philosophy*. Rangoon: British Burma Press, 1909.

Pool, John J. *Studies in Mohammedanism: Historical and Doctrinal, with a Chapter on Islam in England*. Westminster: A. Constable, 1892.

Quilliam, W.H. *The Faith of Islam*. Liverpool: Willmer Bros., 1892.

Quilliam, W.H. *Fanatics and Fanaticism*. Liverpool: Crescent Printing, 1898.

Robinson-Dunn, Diane Liga. *The Harem, Slavery and British Imperial Culture: Anglo-Muslim Relations in the Late Nineteenth Century*. Manchester: Manchester University Press, 2006.

Singleton, Brent D. "'That Ye May Know Each Other': Late Victorian Interactions between British and West African Muslims," *Journal of Muslim Minority Affairs* (forthcoming).

Sterry, Frank W. *H.Y.J.T.: A Brief Biographical Sketch of the Life of Henry Yates Jones Taylor, the Gloucester Historian, Antiquary, Scholar and Poet*. Gloucester: J. Bellows, 1909.

Tyssen, Amherst D. *The Birth of Islam: A Dramatic Poem Showing the Triumph of Faith Over Infidelity, Worldliness, and Bigotry*. London: T. Fisher Unwin, 1895.

Tyssen, Amherst D. *The Life and Teachings of Muhammad*. London: Luzac & Co., 1907.

Tyssen, Amherst D. *Occasional Hymns*. London: [n.p.], 1902.

Wolffe, John, ed. *Religion in Victorian Britain*. Vol. 5, *Culture and Empire*. Manchester: Manchester University Press, 1997.

ABOUT THE EDITOR

BRENT SINGLETON is a Librarian at California State University, San Bernardino. He holds a BA in History and an MLIS from the University of California, Los Angeles. He has written many articles and edited a book (*Yankee Muslim: The Asian Travels of Mohammed Alexander Russell Webb*) on Islam in the United States and Britain during the Victorian Era.

www.ingramcontent.com/pod-product-compliance
Lightning Source LLC
LaVergne TN
LVHW041618070426
835507LV00008B/312